P9-CQV-952

THE TQM TRILOGY

USING
ISO 9000,
———THE———
DEMING PRIZE,
———AND THE———
BALDRIGE AWARD
TO ESTABLISH A SYSTEM
FOR TOTAL QUALITY
MANAGEMENT

FRANCIS X. MAHONEY • CARL G. THOR

amacom
American Management Association

New York • Atlanta • Boston • Chicago • Kansas City • San Francisco • Washington, D.C.
Brussels • Mexico City • Tokyo • Toronto

This publication is designed to provide accurate and authoritative information in regard to the subject matter covered. It is sold with the understanding that the publisher is not engaged in rendering legal, accounting, or other professional service. If legal advice or other expert assistance is required, the services of a competent professional person should be sought.

Library of Congress Cataloging-in-Publication Data

Mahoney, Francis Xavier, 1931–
    The TQM trilogy : using ISO 9000, the Deming Prize, and the
Baldrige Award to establish a system for total quality management /
Francis X. Mahoney. Carl G. Thor.
        p.   cm.
    Includes bibliographical references and index.
    ISBN 0-8144-5105-5
    1. Total quality management.   2. Quality assurance—Management.
3. Quality control—Standards.   4. Malcolm Baldrige National Quality
Award.   I. Thor, Carl G.   II. Title.
HD62.15.M346   1994
658.5'62—dc20   93-40248
                                                              CIP

Printing number

10   9   8   7   6   5   4   3   2   1

Contents

List of Exhibits

Preface

This book is unique. It combines the elements of the three most universally accepted quality models in a new way to provide a foundation for a *quality management transformation*.

This book also is unique because it is **not** about technical quality processes. . . . It **is** a book about organizations and their *management*, which enables introduction and deployment of the best of technical quality processes. It provides a practical framework and the tools needed to get the job done. There is very little philosophy here—and no abstract theory. There are numerous pages of concrete and sensible suggestions, outlines, agendas, checklists, questionnaires, and models born out of years of experience in installing and transforming organizational systems. This is precisely what managers and professionals need: practical tools and down-to-earth approaches to support their vision of a quality culture.

We will argue for the creation and maintenance of a new and improved management system from "day one," bringing the quality system along as the management system matures. Focusing on the "Q" in TQM (which most managers do) is wrong-minded; it is a trap for the unsuspecting. We want to set you straight on what is right-minded: focusing on the "M." What is needed for manager success is total *management* quality, or TMQ. Emphasizing the quality component in an environment that is not supportive of the kinds of actions needed to achieve major breakthroughs in quality is much like "throwing good seed on bad soil." The book will help you with the needed transformations; it pays close attention to managing change.

It is startling that reports indicate around two-thirds of "total *quality* management" initiatives are failing. They do not have to; we know how to avoid failing. Then, too, there seems to be massive hesitation in the face of logic that says DO SOMETHING to enhance competitive strength domestically and internationally. Why do we have bunches of curious spectators, and not enthusiastic activists? Because of lack of familiarity in how to get started in transforming an organization and its management? We can handle that.

Accumulated evidence indicates that some obvious errors are made at the start of change efforts. The most obvious is reaching beyond one's means. That is, companies with few resources and a low level of staff sophistication are well advised to start their improvement efforts where they are. Obvious problems should be tackled with obvious solutions. This book will help: It is designed to be tailorable to specific company situations. Sophisticated companies with generous resources and a high level of staff sophistication can tackle the most difficult improvement challenges. Again, this book will help with its flexible approaches and tailorable tools.

We know that starting is not the whole story—perhaps not even half the story. It is critical to plan where you want to go, and how to get there, at the outset. You must do more. We have what we call the Evergreen System process designed to ensure that a change will last and flourish. Few managers take the time to look ahead and take the essential steps to ensure what they start will last. When the new initiative gets in trouble (usually twelve to eighteen months down the road), it is often too late to retrieve it.

In between planning and creating a vision—and ensuring that the vision remains "evergreen"—there is the actual process of transformation (managing change, if you will) that must be carried out. We have a surefire, simple mechanism to help this happen. We call it the "TQ Triad." It does a great job of introducing change at operating levels.

The book is organized to get its job done in four parts:

1. Creating a Quality *Management* System
2. Tapping the World's Quality Management Wisdom
3. Implementing a Premium Quality Management System
4. Getting Premium Performance From Your Quality Management System

The four parts cover the both the traditional "Plan-Do-Check-Act" model of quality assurance and "Vision-Mission-Goals-Implementation-Evaluation-Adjustment-Recycle" model of a *systems approach* to management.

The three main recommended activities are:

- Sifting through the relevant and applicable management elements of the "TQM Trilogy" (ISO 9000 Standards, the Deming Prize, and the Baldrige Award) to design a quality management system.
- Developing the processes and procedures to implement the system. There are three mechanisms involved: TQManagement (an overall system description and guide to introduction), TQMetrics (a self-tracking measurement log to record ideas and contributions), and TQMeetings (task force and work group guide to working together for quality). This set of three elements is our "TQ Triad."
- Sustaining the system, and helping it flourish through an application of the Evergreen System.

Remember, the secret to success is simply installing a quality *management* system, then a *quality* management system. Too many quality improvement initiatives involve getting out the brass polish, and polishing up a *quality* assurance program. Unfortunately, that won't do it. "New wine in old bottles" simply yields an improved *quality* management process. It does nothing to transform an organization and its culture to a quality *management* system.

One major contribution of the designers of the Baldrige Award model was to enrich technical quality activities by the introduction of organization behavior and development considerations. This created a decent general management model. Baldrige judging helped improve the model continuously by discovering areas that needed to be strengthened. Add the ISO 9000 Standards and the Deming Prize (Japan) model to the Baldrige model, and you have a framework for creating a superb *general management* model. If you want to explore these three resources in detail, ordering instructions for the Baldrige Award Guidelines (free) and ASQC's Q90 series (for a modest cost) are in the related chapters. The Deming Prize checklist is included in the text.

To summarize, *The TQM Trilogy* will provide you with a successful general management model, from which a total quality process can be installed. The book actually does more than this by providing tools for helping you get the culture change job done, and processes to help transform your organization. We urge you to tailor your own quality management system. It *must* reflect the views of your organization's leadership and its competitive and cultural situation. Choices must be made among the alternatives suggested here. Because of the "tool kit" nature of this book, you will be provided with numerous opportunities to think through what is best for your organization and hopefully be able to customize your own quality processes.

This book, then, is totally different from all the other "total quality" books around. It's a unique guide to quality management *success*!

Frank Mahoney
Carl Thor

Houston, Texas
November 1993

Introduction

A seminal study of organizational culture conducted by John P. Kotter and James L. Heskett, and reported in the book *Corporate Culture and Performance*, concluded that effective leadership is fundamental to a successful change to a healthy and adaptive organizational culture. Effective leaders convince people of the existence of a crisis (usually brought about by competition or the business environment), communicate a new corporate vision and a new set of strategies to make that vision a reality, and then motivate others to provide the leadership to implement the necessary changes.

According to Kotter and Heskett, leaders look for quick but sustainable successes and drive cultural change by these initial successful results. Leaders communicate their visions in concrete terms; they make general comments about various constituencies (especially customers) and leadership (denigrating excessive bureaucracy) and specific comments about vital strategies and practices. In almost all cases, they embody the cultures they desire. Their actions give credibility to their words, and their successes make it clear that their words make sense.

A Tool Kit for Leaders

Leaders at all levels need clear, practical, familiar, and easy-to- communicate approaches to make progress. This book is designed to address these challenges and to function as a professional or management tool kit. You will find concrete and sensible suggestions, tips, outlines, checklists, questionnaires, and models. We provide precisely what you leaders need: substantive approaches to support your vision of an effective quality management culture. Instead of simply cheerleading the need for change, we show you how to develop specific visions and concrete strategies to bring it about.

There are four parts and two main activities covered here.

The Parts

The parts cover both the traditional Plan-Do-Check-Act model of quality assurance and the Purpose/Mission-Goals/Targets-Implementation/Evaluation-Adjustment/Accountability-Recycle model of a systems approach to management. They are as follows:

1. Creating a Total Management Quality System
2. Tapping the World's Quality Management Wisdom: The Trilogy
3. Implementing a Total Management Quality System
4. Sustaining Premium Performance With Your Management System

The Activities

The three main activities discussed are:

1. The process of sifting through the relevant and applicable elements of the Total Quality Management (TQM) Trilogy:
   * The ISO 9000/Q90 Standards
   * The Deming Prize
   * The Malcolm Baldrige National Quality Award
     to design and create a total management model.
2. The development of processes and procedures to implement the model. There are three publications involved:
   * *TQManagement*—An overall system guide
   * *TQMetrics*—A self-tracking measurement log
   * *TQMeetings*—A task force and work group guide to working together for quality
   These three mechanisms are called the TQ Triad, about which much will be said throughout the book.
3. The essential steps in introducing and nourishing successful transformations. Evergreen in action.

The Target: A Total *Management* Quality System

Throughout this book, the underlying message is the importance of developing a quality *management* system. A *quality* management system—TQM in the traditional sense—is what we've known for years as a quality assurance program; it is narrow, specialized, and statistical. A quality *management* system includes the quality assurance process as one element, but in addition it is organizationwide, reaches from supplier through processes to customers, involves and empowers all employees, and uses various kinds of data to enhance planning and decision making. The first requirement is to create and maintain a new and improved *management* system; *quality* can then be brought along as the management system matures. There is ample evidence that many quality initiatives have been disappointments because the emphasis was on the quality component without concern for what it takes to make quality flourish and last—a methodology we call the Evergreen System.

The key to success is to use the management experience and expertise found in the TQM Trilogy to create a top-notch management system. Once that is done, the quality component can be added, using the TQ Triad to promote cultural change. Management then provides the strength, substance, and integration needed to make its quality element successful over time.

Most organizations enjoying a modicum of success in the marketplace already have a quality management and management quality program. But just in case, Appendix D outlines a grass-roots start-up quality operation. What may need special attention, however, are the two "people" dimensions and the three "fundamental" program elements involved in today's quality management programs.

People Dimensions

1. Leadership
2. Human resources development and management

Fundamental Program Elements

1. Total involvement (TI), an organizationwide activity
2. Continuous improvement (CI), an ongoing process
3. Customer orientation (CO), an end-user definition of quality performance

This group of three we call TICICO. Remember that term. It appears again in this book. Using these three elements to get started or to breathe new life into an earlier initiative will generate the kind of quality management results most organizations want and need.

Each organization must tailor its own total management quality (TMQ) system to reflect the views of its leadership and its competitive and cultural situation. You must choose between various approaches to defining a quality management system. This book helps you to discover what is best for you.

Part One

Creating a Total Management Quality System

This book does not address a *quality* management system in the sense of TQM but rather a quality *management* system—meaning total *management* quality (TMQ). Why the change in emphasis? Too many "total quality" projects have failed. One common denominator of failure seems to be a lack of the supporting management system elements—not to mention management culture—needed to obtain initial success and maintain that success over time.

But there is a deeper reason for this failure, and it is rooted in management history. Despite fragmentary efforts, management activities and processes were not codified until about thirty years ago. Until that time, there was no such thing as a comprehensive management system. It was not until the later 1960s that Rensis Likert began to devote a large part of his professional life to codifying and optimizing general management systems. His well-known 1967 work, *The Human Organization: Its Management and Value*, was a monumental effort to define an effective management system. Likert's system worked, and a major oil refinery and several automobile and electronics organizations benefited significantly. But why didn't the system spread? Well, the model was too demanding with its benchmarking and ongoing quantified assessments, and it was too systematic with its specification of the kind of culture that supports excellence. It was too intrusive of leaders because it required their continual involvement in improvement.

Time has finally caught up with Rensis Likert. Now we find that many of his concepts not only *can* be used to install and maintain quality management systems but *must* be.

Today there exists an incredible opportunity to improve management systems. We have three broadly accepted models designed to promote and improve quality: the ISO 9000 Standards, the Deming Prize, and the Malcolm Baldrige National Quality Award. Each model has general management dimensions that when pulled together provide a Holy Grail for those who want to establish total management quality. Together, they constitute the TQM Trilogy.

Why rely on the TQM Trilogy? Because it offers a tremendous collection of management wisdom. There is also worldwide awareness of its components and broad acceptance of its elements.

Characteristics of the TQM Trilogy

- The Trilogy furnishes an efficient, effective management system launch vehicle, which provides an excellent opportunity to save time and money while achieving a rapid, confident cultural modification.
- It makes best use of available organizational expertise and experience; it proceeds from existing successes in management and quality assurance.
- It can be readily tailored for almost any organization in any sector; it has universal management qualities.
- It goes well beyond the exclusive profit orientation of conventional management analysis; it applies in a wide range of sectors.
- It ensures early success because it builds on valid and proven methods and procedures that are easily communicated.

Part One sets the scene by detailing the planning activities needed and establishing the Evergreen System—the process that will enable your system to last over the long haul (see Chapter 11).

1

Scoping Your Management System

Market share is a major factor in profitability, and it is largely determined by quality. International competition continues to erode market share, and increased consumer sensitivity to quality here at home exacerbates the situation.

But there's more. For-profit companies can benefit far beyond market share, and not-for-profit organizations can also benefit significantly.

How?

The way you do business is positively affected by quality concepts—e.g., deploying a quality culture throughout the organization, paying attention to continuous improvement, and focusing on results. Significant knowledge exists on how to improve overall management effectiveness. That knowledge has to do with installing processes and structures that improve not only market share but operational performance, employee (or associate) relations, supplier performance, and customer (or client) focus and satisfaction. Total management quality systems also have significant potential for generating internal excitement, improving day-to-day communication, developing a common vocabulary, enhancing teamwork, sensitizing managers and supervisors to employees' contributions, and expanding the uses of feedback.

The real key, however, is the management system surrounding quality efforts. For a quality system to succeed, the organization's management system must be top-notch. Too many organizations have been frustrated, and too many quality system installations have failed, simply because the emphasis was on quality and not on management. The lesson to be learned from past errors and excesses in efforts to create quality systems is this: The only way to obtain a high-benefit yield from your investment of time and resources is to focus first on the organization's management system and then bring quality system improvements along with management system improvements.

Preliminary Considerations

About now you may be thinking about the currently popular chaos theory that says that not everything is linear, that lots of things in systems happen simultaneously. It *is* hard to track cause and effect. Things *do* look chaotic, but there really are causal relationships between what appear to be random relationships. The more we can observe and measure, the less chaotic things seem. Unfortunately, we just can't observe or measure them with today's techniques.

Starting anything new takes a lot of energy and talent, and starting anything new in an organization takes careful planning. One key to effective planning is to ask yourself the right questions. That way you can surface all the issues you'll eventually have to deal with. Here are seven key questions that you should ask yourself. The answers, no matter what they are, will prove valuable now by helping you focus your energies and resources. They will continue to be useful as the TMQ approach unfolds:

1. How do you think people in your organization will respond to the need for quality management goals and continuous improvement on a long-term basis?
2. What are the specific organizational conditions and objectives that should motivate creation of a quality management system (QMS)?
3. Is your organization under pressure from customers to document or improve quality? What must you do?
4. Does your organization have solid information about the needs and expectations of its customers, both internal and external? If not, what can be done to remedy the situation?
5. What will it take to obtain the commitment of your employees or associates to undertake new or expanded quality management and quality system initiatives? Who should handle this?
6. Is your organization's culture accepting of empowerment? Remember, while *involvement* is a familiar term in most organizations, *empowerment* means something a lot stronger in terms of authorized actions.
7. Is your organization ready for the "wall-to-wall" attention to quality, on a continuous basis and with high standards and

superior results, that is needed for it to be a world-class organization?

Every organization needs management objectives in order for it to run effectively. Here are some examples:

Objectives Typically Associated With TMQ

- Continual attention to quality, productivity, and organizational performance
- Understanding of domestic and international economic challenges
- Gaining and maintaining a competitive edge
- Employee or associate acceptance of new performance initiatives
- Empowerment of individual and team contributions to quality
- Enhanced accountability through measurement and comparison with others
- Sharpened focus on internal and external customers to improve interfaces

Although these objectives and others may be desirable, a TMQ system has certain requirements that are difficult to achieve, at least quickly (most organizations install quality mechanisms in phases and through a pilot program strategy). Here are some examples:

TMQ Requirements

- Know and meet the customer's expectations and requirements on time, the first time, 100 percent of the time.
- Manage by prevention rather than inspection; recognize that quality can't be "inspected in."
- Place significant pressure on supplier quality; build closer supplier relationships.
- Measure quality costs; use "benchmarking" and "metrics" to prove that prevention and empowerment are the optimum cost options.
- Manage the introduction of the management system and related changes carefully (take the time to do it right).
- Train for appropriate levels of competence in organizational and quality skills.
- Prepare people to take action to ensure quality; enhance procedural guides.
- Strive for selected major improvements and overall performance at world-class levels.

Can you handle these kinds of requirements? They are fundamental to TMQ creation and maintenance.

Are you ready to espouse the kinds of values needed for TMQ? Here are some examples:

- Equitable and ethical leadership
- Horizontal and vertical communication and coordination
- Employee/associate empowerment and recognition
- Training and development in general and in quality methods in particular
- Encouragement of innovation and risk taking
- Assurance of safety and environmental protection
- A culture of continuous improvement and focus on the future
- Effective customer relations and guarantees
- Effective supplier relations and planning participation
- Long-term decision horizons

A TMQ installation almost always involves paradigm shifts. A paradigm is simply a model or example of sorts; in the context of our business literature a "paradigm shift" has come to mean a *huge change*. Here are some paradigm shifts you might encounter:

- Using a system to measure and achieve customer satisfaction; the customer (external or internal) becomes a key success criterion.
- Installing methods for continuous improvement of all organizational processes on an integrated basis.
- Involving employees at all levels in achieving quality and empowering them to act to ensure quality.
- Moving toward team management, with a reduction in the number of supervisors and supervisory levels.
- Changing traditional human resources systems to create an egalitarian, nonintimidating culture.
- Taking enough care and time in your installation to get it right.

Having considered the kinds of changes, or paradigm shifts, that you will encounter, let's continue to energize your TMQ by identifying three sweeping steps. This is where you begin your system design. But common sense will dictate the size and rate of change involved.

The Basic Approach to Creating a TMQ System

Most important for success is having a practical, easy-to-install overall concept—one that will work and last. The following is a simple, straightforward approach to system design consisting of three elements: (1) handling the preparation, (2) establishing system content, and (3) creating an implementation and maintenance process.

Handling the Preparation

Seven preparatory steps need to be performed before you can complete your system design:

1. Establish a strategic plan or review the existing plan for appropriate management quality and quality management targets.
2. Develop your quality management mission and objectives.
3. Assess the organization's management quality and quality management status.
4. Ensure integration with existing plans or planning.
5. Identify cross-functional task force opportunities.
6. Develop input/feedback from those who will be involved.
7. Integrate Evergreen System elements for acceptance and maintenance—that is, those elements that will keep the system "fresh" over the long term. As discussed in Chapter 2 and more fully in Chapter 11, this must be done *now*. To make the system *last*, these elements must be put in place *first*.

Establishing System Content

Today there are three widely accepted management models that can be integrated and synthesized to create a highly credible and profitable management system: the ISO 9000 Standards, the Deming Prize, and the Malcolm Baldrige National Quality Award, which make up the TQM Trilogy. The Trilogy strategy is to identify and integrate useful quality management dimensions of all three.

ISO 9000 Series Standards

In 1987, the International Standards Organization (ISO) created the ISO 9000 Series of quality standards. Companies that meet these standards can register as ISO 9000 companies. More than 10,000 company sites are registered in over thirty nations. The ISO 9000 Series intends to stimulate trade by providing third-party assurance of an organization's ability to meet specifications and perform to negotiated standards. The focus is on basic organization and policy in regard to quality. However, because there is little concern about how the organization chooses to manage itself and its customer relations, ISO 9000 certification cannot be used to imply that a company is best, elite, or world-class.

The Deming Prize

The Deming Prize was created by the Japanese Union of Scientists and Engineers (JUSE) in 1951 to honor W. Edwards Deming, who contributed greatly to Japan's post-World War II recovery and its adoption and standard use of quality principles.

The Deming Prize is not an annual contest; it is recognition that an organization has attained a certain quality standard. Following an indefinite period (typically from two to five years) of coaching by JUSE consultants, an applicant for the Prize is assigned a team of examiners who interpret both the organization's current business situation and the status of a series of checklist items (Particulars). There is no limit on the number of winners in any year.

The most intriguing feature of the Particulars is that there is no mention of customer satisfaction. The emphasis is on rigorous statistical approaches and aggressive problem solving throughout the line operation of the organization.

The Malcolm Baldrige National Quality Award

The Malcolm Baldrige National Quality Award, named after former, and popular, secretary of commerce Malcolm Baldrige, who pushed for a U.S. quality award as part of a national strategy to increase U.S. quality competitiveness, was created by an act of Congress in 1987 to stimulate quality awareness in the United States. It was the result of several years of patient development (and lobbying) by quality organizations such as the American Productivity and Quality Center (APQC) and the American Society for Quality Control (ASQC), and by many dedicated individual quality professionals. Funding for the Award process comes from a private foundation created for that purpose by interested companies and individuals. The Award is administered by a private-sector agent (currently the ASQC); the judges and examiners are drawn mostly from private-sector companies. In any year, there can be a maximum of two winners in each of three categories (manufacturing, service, and small business).

Candidates are judged according to seven major criteria categories, twenty-eight subcriteria categories (Examination Items), and eighty-nine specific Areas to Address as currently constructed. Unlike the two other parts of the Trilogy, the Award places greatest emphasis on customer satisfaction. There are few mandatory "techniques," but winning essentially requires a substantial "prevention" orientation. One somewhat controversial requirement is the effort a company is expected to put into benchmarking its level of organizational performance. A strong improvement trend alone may not be sufficient for a high score if starting levels of performance were low.

Judgment is made on approach, deployment, and results. Approach considers the methods used: Are they prevention-based, effective, and well measured and evaluated? Deployment requires total quality management throughout the organization—not only on the plant floor but in support areas and offices. Results include quality level and trend, evidence of sustained improvement (not just over the previous year), and a demonstrable link between quality practice and result.

The TQM Trilogy Hypothesis

The TQM Trilogy hypothesis is that selectively picking quality management elements from the Standards, the Prize, and the Award makes good sense. These management elements represent some of the best organization- or company-level management thinking ever formalized. Instead of sponsoring research at great cost and consumption of energy, managers can "cherry pick" elements from models that are widely accepted, albeit uncritically and not well researched. The MBNQA, for example, is continuously improved, and its Guidelines are changed annually. Picking relevant elements and creating an appropriately comprehensive management model are twin challenges, but they will save you time, effort, and expense—although not mental effort. From the Trilogy elements, you can create checklists with which to build a Master Manual (see later in this chapter) describing the operation of your chosen (or preferred) management systems.

Here's how we see the three pieces fitting together: The Baldrige is the most far-reaching and broad-range source. The ISO 9000 Series adds detail at operating levels. The Deming Prize adds numerous opportunities for sophisticated statistical treatments.

Other Quality Criteria

You should add any professional or state-level government quality criteria that are important to you. Check other lesser known and emerging quality initiatives as appropriate (see Appendix C).

The Master Manual Concept

Select appropriate elements, often SOPs, and create a Master Manual that will support your quality management mission. It is interesting to note that ISO 9004, which specifically covers management of a quality system, presents a quality manual as the way to record and distribute SOPs relative to the registration process. The people who preaudit and audit will continually turn to the quality manual to see how thorough and complete your quality procedures are, and they will pull pages and go right into your operation to see if your employees are performing according to the SOPs. For our part, we have used the Master Manual concept in a much broader fashion.

The Master Manual functions as a protocol for organizational change. It provides direction, priorities, and approvals to which people can turn if they find themselves in a situation that conflicts with history or other organizational elements. In the technology of managing change, this makes the Master Manual a very useful tool. Every organization's Manual will look different, at least in terms of size and scope, but generally, it builds from the unit level, where there may be a handful of pages, to the top levels of an organization, where there may be a series of binders. See Chapter 6 for more detail on how to include suggested forms for tracking processes and procedures.

The criterion for inclusion of an element is how it supports your organization's mission and business plan. There must also be a way to factor in "rolling adjustments" as experience is gained and the dimensions of the Standards, Prize, and Award are improved over time. (See Chapters 3–5 for expanded descriptions of the contributions available from the three Trilogy elements.)

After you have selected the appropriate elements, prepare composite and unit-level quality standards to give substance and focus to your system. Design and use tracking sheets to document progress.

Creating an Implementation and Maintenance Process

The quality management approach must be easy to grasp and attractive to operating managers. Beware of excessive detail and cumbersome administrative requirements. The three recommended sets of materials—TQManagement (master description), TQMetrics (individual log), and TQMeetings (team and task force methods)—make up the TQ Triad.

The TQ Triad

1. *TQManagement* is "the book"—philosophy, goals, concepts, organization—generated by the company on local approaches to comprehensive quality management. It is a thirty-five- to forty–page illustrated publication that communicates such topics as purposes, philosophy, organization, improvement methods, and statistics.

2. *TQMetrics* is an individual log, a pocket notebook used to record both measurements and ideas, that generally moves with the person to

whom it belongs. Although a computer spreadsheet can be adapted to TQMetrics to track ideas and contributions, a practical, take-it-along format is essential if mainstream operating and field people are to use it.

3. *TQMeetings* is a company-generated set of materials that support quality teams and task forces in their various activities and relationships (horizontally and vertically). The package includes such things as explanations of meeting types, objectives, and schedules; meeting methods and techniques; tips for problem solving and planning; and teamwork assessment instruments. Team-based systems need support; few can run on their own energy.

This basic three-part model provides operating managers with the simple, easily communicated approach to "doing" quality management that they want and need. It presents a clear picture of a complete quality system and shows a clear path to follow to bring it into existence. It really is all that is needed for change at the operational level.* It is also practical, inexpensive, and amenable to local preparation and tailoring.

To introduce the process, set up three phases:

1. The *launch* phase, in which essential communication, training, and planning take place, along with selected pilot activities.
2. One or more *operational* phases, until the system becomes part of the everyday routine.
3. A *feedback* and *review* phase. The process will most likely need revision and recycling, since the quality management philosophy espoused by most executives and managers is to improve continuously toward a world-class capability.

The Importance of Planning to System Success

In order to start a formal quality management effort in an organization that has never had one, it is clearly necessary to plan what is to be done. Where will this effort begin? What is the role of senior managers? Who carries the day-to-day coordination responsibility? What tools and techniques will be brought in and taught, and over what time frame? How will the effort be communicated, and by whom? Who decides priorities?

In the past, quality improvement was often grafted onto an existing management process by loosely authorized advocates who could exer-

*The raging debate about changing performance appraisal processes and switching to a full team management approach will not be addressed here. *You do not need* these kinds of cultural changes to achieve quality *management* and *quality* management.

cise personal leadership. In essence, operating or line management took full responsibility for grass-roots improvement. This was a good thing; much useful change was achieved by individuals who took the bit in their teeth. Increasingly, however, the quality effort is being initiated by top management in a systematic manner, casting informal advocates in roles of natural helpers rather than champions. This is one time that leadership must take an active role.

Today, line and staff management routinely take their main direction from quality elements in their organizations' strategic and operating plans, elements which are eventually integrated into routine business plans. Thus, it is common to hear quality managers or staff specialists say that their goal is to "work themselves out of a job." In other words, any formal role initially required to establish a quality management process should become unnecessary within a few years as quality management becomes fully absorbed into the routine thought processes of line and staff managers.

In the intermediate time period, great attention needs to be given to integrating quality considerations and the planning process, most frequently through a quality improvement assessment project. An early step in most formal improvement efforts is to assess the quality improvement potential of the organization using the criteria associated with the Baldrige Award. However, a Trilogy-based instrument could certainly be designed.

Priority targets of the quality improvement process must support the key targets of the strategic and operational plans. This lays the groundwork for the eventual "disappearance" of special quality management planning through absorption into the business planning process.

Strategic or long-range planning (with a time horizon of five or more years) is a key to success for many organizations. If quality management is central to the successful operation of an organization and takes a number of years to install, then blending quality management into strategic planning becomes absolutely essential. Short-range planning, essentially the same process as long-range planning, generally has a time horizon of one year. Quality considerations should be blended into the annual operating plan as well.

Quality Management Planning Process

Assessment Steps:

1. Establish purpose and goals of the management system.
2. Assess organization's strengths, weaknesses, opportunities, dangers.

3. Develop tentative key planning issues.
4. Evaluate, consolidate, and prioritize the issues.
5. Designate selected *final planning issues*.

Decision Steps (for all final planning issues):

6. Develop alternative routes and channels to goal achievement through such activities as extrapolation, simulation, gaming, and brainstorming.
7. Evaluate the alternatives against the forecast environment or climate; determine impact; adjust.
8. Decide upon best alternatives(s) or combine alternatives to optimize outcomes; identify interface considerations.
9. Assemble a tentative plan (e.g., detailing who, what, and when); apply Evergreen concepts.
10. Resolve internal organizational conflicts.
11. Approve *final action plan(s)*.

Implementation Steps (for each approved final action plan element):

12. Develop contingent programs and budgets for each action plan element.
13. *Do it* (or a pilot if appropriate).
14. Monitor and control results; check against your Evergreen model.
15. Evaluate feedback against purpose, goals.
16. Recycle as appropriate.

Well, that was a rough trip, but a necessary one. We have a concept of a quality management system, and an overview of how to bring it into existence. Next, we'll dive directly in to the challenging business of managing organizational transitions, flesh out the system components to be transitioned, and find ways to ensure that what is transitioned endures.

2

From a Solid Launch to the Evergreen System

Once you've roughed out a plan for establishing your management system, there are four steps to take:

1. Examine the question of whether to alter your organization's culture before installing the TMQ or to install the system and alter the culture as you go along.
2. Develop basic skills in how to change organizations (and individuals).
3. Establish the TMQ launch and operational phases.
4. Work through the Evergreen System.

Altering the Culture

How do you define an existing organization culture? According to authors John P. Kotter and James P. Heskett in *Corporate Culture and Performance*, an organization culture is made up of (1) shared values (e.g., important concerns and goals) that tend to shape group behavior and persist over time and (2) group behavior norms (e.g., actions that are rewarded or punished) that persist because group members teach the practices to new members. The shared values tend to be invisible and hard to change; the group behavior norms tend to be visible and easier to change.

Corporate culture will become an even more important factor in long-term economic performance well into the twenty-first century; the major issues will be dealing with tolerance of inappropriate behavior and resistance to change. We believe that although cultures are difficult

18

to change, they can be made more performance-enhancing. Cultural change is complex, takes time, and requires leadership; that leadership needs a realistic vision of existing values and behaviors if it is to be effective in instituting change.

When creating a new or revised system you must first decide whether to create content and structure for the new system or attend to process and culture. The pragmatic answer is to do both at once. You could start with a formal assessment, perhaps using a survey. But you may not be able to detect relevant and important cultural dimensions and demands until you begin installing the quality management system. If you *really* want to know an organization, try to change it. Places where the system and the culture clash will become obvious instantly.

Making vague efforts to change the culture without some clear notion of what the result should be may pose certain problems. Organizational elements may flounder and never acquire a clear focus; you may be tempted to turn to, and thus become dependent on, outside consulting help. Also, you may create "loose cannons," people with sharply different views and definitions of effective values and behavioral norms.

It is better to go forward with clear and substantive initiatives and respond to your culture in the context of system creation and maintenance. You will quickly encounter some important and specific cultural issues. The Baldrige Award criteria have been carefully crafted to deal with mainstream cultural considerations, emphasizing as they do such issues as building or confirming quality performance values, disseminating useful information, training in quality technology, and recognizing individual and team contributions.

The Award also speaks directly to developing work groups to pursue quality and performance objectives. Thus, there is attention to relatively concrete cultural dimensions such as involvement, empowerment, innovation, evaluation, and the creation of high-performance teams. These dimensions are manageable, sensible, and consistent with modern practice. Consider whether your culture supports them or not.

Changing People and Processes

Before you undertake an initiative involving significant change, you should first evaluate how ready your organization is for it. The following questions will help with the assessment:

Assessing Readiness for Change
- To what extent do people see your organization as a top-notch operation and a good place to work? If this is *not* the current

perception, what are the implications for installing and maintaining a quality management system?

- Do employees/associates understand the Pacific Rim and European Community trade challenges and their potential organizational consequences?
- How would you describe your culture with respect to product or service quality? Is it valued? In what sense? By whom? To what effect?
- Do management-level people accept today's push for quality and the drive for continuous quality improvement? Are there champions of quality? Who are they?
- Is there a quality improvement buy-in at the lowest levels of the organization? How does the union (if any) come out on the subject of quality? What are the implications?
- Who shapes and refines the culture in your organization? What is management's role with respect to culture, and what is the employee's/associate's role? On balance, does one group have more impact than the other? What are the consequences?
- Is the organization receptive to change? What was the last significant change? How did it go? What can be learned from previous experiences?
- What organizational strengths exist that support a quality management system installation and operation? Are there relevant initiatives already under way that should be integrated with new initiatives?
- What weaknesses must be acknowledged and considered in order to move forward successfully? List needed corrective actions and who should be responsible for dealing with the situations.
- Are people aware that installation and maintenance of a quality management system are highly demanding in terms of the need for skilled leadership and human resources contributions?

If the answers to these questions turn out to be negative, your best use of time and resources is to not go forward with a new quality management system (QMS).* Instead, work on leadership and motivation practices; communicate the competitive environment; build cus-

---

*However, one MBNQA winner saw the process underlying the Award as a way to offset severe international economic challenges and decided to plow ahead on the basis that a current lack of employee acceptance was more acceptable than not acting at all. This is not desirable, but it works. Management simply has to live with the hard feelings that result and work toward patching things up. If the organization survives as a result of the drastic action, people tend to be forgiving.

tomer service values internally and externally; identify managers and employees who "buy in" to the need for change; recognize and act on cultural elements that are blocking change; assess your company's previous experiences with significant change (and the continuing consequences); inventory current strengths and weaknesses; and alert people to the challenges that lie ahead.

If the answers to these questions are positive, you can proceed to the following step-by-step model for managing change in individuals or organizations:

1. *Prioritize your objectives.* Start with key elements of your plans. You must know what you want to accomplish.

2. *Conduct a force field analysis (Exhibit 2-1) to assist in your choice of strategy.* This analysis examines forces that support (drive) or oppose (restrain) transitions so that you can identify and choose alternatives and evaluate their consequences. Here are the recommended steps:

   a. List your driving forces (see Exhibit 2-1). These might include the economic environment, a sense of competition, or your own personal leadership.
   b. Do the same for your restraining forces (Exhibit 2-1). These might include earlier unhappy experiences with change, your own rigidity, or employee/associate concerns about the motives involved.
   c. Rank the driving and restraining forces in terms of their significance for quality management system (QMS) introduction and maintenance.
   d. Reduce or eliminate the restraining forces.* Why? Because if you try to push change with driving forces alone, you will breed resistance (for every action, there is an equal and opposite reaction). Do not abandon application of the drivers, but recognize that they are almost always biased in favor of the organization and its management. Restraining forces are usually in touch with employee/associate needs, interests, and values.
   e. Don't try to get everything settled at once. It may make sense to take your time in working out a transition. Plan-Do-Check-Act is a common quality control model. It also works here.
   f. Evaluate progress in terms of mission and objectives. (See Exhibit 8-4 for additional problem-solving techniques.)

---

*Watch this point; it may not fit your biases.

Exhibit 2-1. Force-field analysis worksheet.

Mission/Plan: _____

_____

_____

Objective(s): _____

_____

_____

	Driving Forces	*Restraining Forces*
Employee/Associate Commitment	1. _____	_____
	2. _____	_____
	3. _____	_____
	4. _____	_____
	5. _____	_____
Financial/Other Resources	1. _____	_____
	2. _____	_____
	3. _____	_____
	4. _____	_____
	5. _____	_____
Customer Acceptance	1. _____	_____
	2. _____	_____
	3. _____	_____
	4. _____	_____
	5. _____	_____

	Driving Forces	*Restraining Forces*
Production of Products/Services	1. _____	_____
	2. _____	_____
	3. _____	_____
	4. _____	_____
	5. _____	_____
Quality Management Techniques	1. _____	_____
	2. _____	_____
	3. _____	_____
	4. _____	_____
	5. _____	_____
Human Resources Management System	1. _____	_____
	2. _____	_____
	3. _____	_____
	4. _____	_____
	5. _____	_____
Other	1. _____	_____
	2. _____	_____
	3. _____	_____
	4. _____	_____
	5. _____	_____

3. Use the following five steps to initiate and maintain change. They may be combined in order to achieve a particular objective:

  a. Create awareness by providing information about new or altered directions and related changes. These could include employee/

associate meetings or articles in company publications (see the section on communication below). Although this activity is essential, it is not particularly powerful. Consider that we know that certain health-related practices (e.g., overeating) are not good for us; but still we persist in them.

b. Ensure organizationwide involvement in planning and problem solving for system issues and activities. New or expanded delegation will empower people to take action. Conducting off-site decision-making meetings for various levels of management is an inherently powerful transition strategy. Breaking away from the ordinary fosters creativity and reduces distractions, and, depending upon distance, makes it slightly harder for people to be called back to the office. Electronics, of course, are always with us.

c. Provide training and development and possibly a broad education effort. Develop and deliver appropriate curricula for various needs; plan informal coaching opportunities. Make sure that what is learned is applied, monitored, and reinforced (see Appendix B for a training model).

d. Recognize and reinforce target behaviors. Identify individuals and teams that demonstrate them and do something to reward that behavior. Check reactions carefully. For example, technicians on a pipeline had a reputation for dismissing letters acknowledging good work. But it turned out that the superficial reactions were not the only reactions; the letters were actually taken home to show to spouses and kids. Invisible third parties became a part of the recognition process.

e. Confront individuals or units with a direct request that certain activities be undertaken (this need not be done in an unfriendly or distant way). Involve management authority, and issue written policies and procedures. The ISO 9000 series is strong on standardized procedures.

4. Allocate resources so that transition strategies can accomplish their objectives. It is important that transition activities be loaded for success in terms of budget, people, and other needs. Leadership is a critical issue; it is imperative to seek out "naturals"—leaders who are convinced in advance that the transition is a must and who have a solid reputation with employees/associates. Those who write about introducing TQM often use the term *champion* to describe the natural quality management leader.

Special transition mechanisms are usually established in the form of task forces and quality teams (see Chapter 8). Existing work groups can become quality teams with an enhancement of their mission and objectives.

Some Shorthand

For convenience, we need to encode the system concepts that are being presented. The initials Q(uality) M(anagement) S(ystem) seem to make a lot of sense. Let's start using them now.

Some Tough Questions

Starting anything new takes a lot of energy and talent, and starting anything new in an organization takes careful planning. One key to effective planning is to ask yourself the right questions. That way you can have the issues you'll eventually have to deal with all in one place. Here are seven key questions that you should ask yourself. The answers, no matter what they are, will prove valuable by helping you focus your energies and resources. They will continue to be useful as the QMS approach unfolds:

1. How do you think people in your organization will respond to the need for quality management goals and continuous improvement on a long-term basis?
2. What are the specific organizational conditions and objectives that should motivate creation of a QMS?
3. Is your organization under pressure from customers to document or improve quality? What must you do?
4. Does your organization have solid information about the needs and expectations of its customers, both internal and external? If not, what can be done to remedy the situation?
5. What will it take to obtain the commitment of your employees/ associates to undertake new or expanded quality management and quality system initiatives? Who should handle this?
6. Is your organization's culture accepting of empowerment? Remember, while *involvement* is a familiar term in most organizations, *empowerment* means something a lot stronger in terms of authorized actions.
7. Is your organization ready for the "wall to wall" attention to quality, on a continuous basis and with high standards and superior results, that is needed for it to be a world-class organization?

Development of a QMS is doable on a self-help basis.

Launch Phase

Note: This is an overview. For more detail see Part Three. The intent at this time is to present an outline of the entire process for ready reference.

1. Have company leaders convene senior-level discussions (probably off-site) and agree on decision support framework in advance, using the following model agenda:

Launch Phase
Executive-Level Model Agenda

- Quality Management Models
  —Experiences available through publications and professional associations
  —Definitions
  —Challenges to be anticipated
  —Current culture and how it is relevant to quality management mission
- Decisions as to specific quality management activities and timing—aided by Decision Aids (ranking instruments, inventories, surveys)
- Detailed Planning for System Operations (using change management tools)
  —Introduction
  —Expansion
  —Maintenance
  —Problem solving, as needed
  —Benchmarking philosophy
- Decisions as to:
  —TQM Trilogy activities
  —TQ Triad preparation
  —Time lines
  —Communications
  —Training
- Key agreements as to Task Forces, Teams
  —Overall strategy
  —Utilization
  —Leadership

—Reporting channels
—Training
—Cross-functional coordination
- Communication Process Requirements
- Training Process Requirements
- Evergreen System (Making Change Last) Considerations
- Follow-Up (Subsequent Meetings, Continuation, Expansion)

---

2. Cascade decision agreements and TMQ process downward.
3. Conduct departmental/division-level meetings (recommended off-site) using the following model agenda:

Department/Division Level/Model Agenda

- Develop understanding and agreement on desirable future courses of action:
  —Establish a quality management vision and mission.
  —Determine tentative launch plans and timing.
  —Respond to initial use of quality status assessment form and recommend future potential use.
- Outline plan for QMS introduction expansion and maintenance:
  —Solve problems as needed.
  —Apply change management model
- Define key people rules:
  —Who will "champion" the activities?
- Establish task forces needed at the outset; describe task force team implementation.
- Develop a plan for interaction to share experiences among major departments and field locations to include cross-functional exchanges.
- Define appropriate interactions with collective bargaining units.
- Integrate historical quality assurance and suggestion system elements with related initiatives.
- Define communication process requirements.
- Identify training needs for all levels and locations. Create a tentative curriculum. (Appendix B applies at management/professional level.)

---

4. Implement Evergreen System elements.
5. Look ahead to system operations phases (covered in detail in Chapter 10).

- Employ the TQ Triad as change protocol (see Chapter 9).
  —*TQManagement*—Philosophy, overall concept publication examples, tailored by organization
  —*TQMetrics*—Individual log tailored by organizational unit
  —*TQMeetings*—Implementation vehicle; supports meeting process tailored by level for task forces and work groups
- Generate planning schedules for events for management and all employees, associates.
- Provide continuous feedback and continuous improvement.
  —Track Evergreen System elements.
  —Incorporate benchmarking.
  —Review, revise, and recycle.
- Ensure accountability via specific reporting mechanisms.

---

6. Back on site, prepare initial edition of Master Manual. One manual should be prepared for each significant organizational unit, listing details on progress targeted, completed, and yet to be done. The Manual percolates upward, with each senior level having its own components as well as summaries from subordinate units. Logically, lowest-level manuals may be very brief.
7. Use the TQM Trilogy—ISO 9000, Deming Prize, and the Malcolm Baldrige Award documentation—as a resource for materials, procedures, and standards to be incorporated in the Manual.
8. Prepare and distribute the three-part TQ Triad discussed in Chapter 1: TQManagement (an organizationwide quality management system description), TQMetrics (a measurement procedures document to give direction and purpose to your quality system), and TQMeetings tools to guide task forces and work groups in quality management activities.
9. Institute your launch strategy and process; go operational when appropriate to achieve your quality management mission/objectives.
10. Obtain feedback. Check and benchmark. Review functions. Revise processes and practices as needed. Recycle.
11. Improve continuously toward world-class management.

Communication Strategies

Remember, transitions are smoothed by communications. Channels can be formal or informal, and there are numerous media options as well. It is helpful to review them from time to time to make sure that the most effective technology or technology combinations are being used. Informal channels always exist, and generally they work faster than formal channels, a prime example being the grapevine, or "rumor mill."

Every communication process should consider the adequacy of upward, as well as downward, flow. Review your options and plan your communication activities so that they support your quality management system.

What key communication channels do you have at your disposal? How will each one influence attitudes and opinions? Are they universally effective? If so, why? If not, why not?

Some Things to Consider

- Is it okay to sway employees/associates toward a particular point of view? If so, in what way? If not, why?
- "Management should be spontaneous and quick in communicating to employees/associates." Accurate? Inaccurate? Why?
- What kinds of communication media are generally available to management? How are they best employed? Describe and critique at least five options, explaining why each is effective or ineffective at your location.
- Credibility and timeliness are two major virtues (and challenges) in organizational communication. How do you achieve and sustain both during a quality system installation?

Training Strategies

Training is vital to bringing about successful transitions. On the one hand, learning about new processes and procedures enables employees and associates to perform as desired and empowers them to take new actions. On the other hand, training can be difficult to conduct; you need a qualified staff and must take the time to do it well. It is essential that a training needs analysis be conducted to ensure that the training hits the right targets, transfers successfully to the job, and makes the best use of the organization's time and other resources. See Appendix B now for training options.

Making Change Last: The Evergreen System

The key to making any system installation successful—and *lasting*—is to consider at the start two major organizational issues: (1) system qualities (or process) and (2) system structure. Too many people charge ahead to design and install a system without ever considering what it takes for a system to last over the long haul—to make it Evergreen.

Why do we use the word *evergreen*? Well, because an evergreen tree has some formidable characteristics, such as:

- It keeps its leaves for several years.
- It grows new leaves before losing its old ones.
- It is tougher and more resilient than other trees.
- It can easily handle temperature changes.
- It is loaded with chlorophyll, and, therefore, creates nourishment for itself readily.

These are also top-notch characteristics for a quality management system.

Chapter 11 has complete coverage of the Evergreen System, but here are the basics:

Evergreen System Qualities
- Congruence with organizational mission, purpose, charter
- Leadership that understands all implications of transitions (e.g., stress, frustrations, shortages)
- Ability to handle tough, challenging objectives and goals
- Consistent owner/investor interests
- Good fit with current climate and environment
- Tested against anticipated future situations
- Ability to attract commitment, interest, and innovation by people who will be affected
- Clear pluses for the organization; a sound rationale for a culture shift
- Good fit with organizational rhythms and calendar (two to five years ahead)
- Involvement and empowerment for key players
- Psychological value to those impacted and expected to contribute
- Recognition opportunities for all
- Potential for obtaining sought-after rewards
- Initial activities that are loaded for success; strengths that are inventoried and integrated
- Realistic time demands and schedules

Evergreen System Structures

- Stable and committed senior leadership
- Champions identified
- A well-defined process, with model(s)
- "Public" organizational commitments
- Planning system in place, with key dates known
- Budget process activated, with controls established
- Progress/process reviews, defined as to content, schedule, and expected follow-up
- Established stewardship results and methods
- Measurement and evaluation processes (e.g., metrics, benchmarks)
- Organizational entities, task forces, teams
- Policies and procedures, with special attention paid to human resources management requirements
- Linkages between internal and external (e.g., supplier, customer) entities
- Protocols for solving problems and managing interfaces; steps for integrating learning
- Operational communication program
- Accessible resources

Even with all these Evergreen qualities and structures in place, it can be tough to get a senior manager to "buy in" to almost anything new or expanded unless the following characteristics are present:

- *Simplicity*—It won't collapse of its own weight.
- *Flexibility*—Commitments are not written in stone.
- *Completeness*—All the bases are covered.
- *Workability*—It's tangible.
- *Appropriateness, Decision Horizon*—It's not at the "far fringe."
- *Acceptability*—It meets with the approval of all or most of the organization.
- *Communicability*—It's easy to understand and "sell."
- *Timeliness*—It fits organizational rhythms (e.g., doesn't disturb accounting during year-end closing).
- *Conservative appearance*—It won't raise the specter of reckless spending.

Recap

Many people have had trouble with total quality/continuous improvement initiatives simply because they lacked the necessary background.

Pay close attention to the tools provided in Part One; they can make the difference between success and failure.

- The key to the successful introduction and maintenance of a quality management system is successful management of the transitions involved.
- Transitions are best accomplished by applying a model that considers available alternatives, ranks alternatives as to effectiveness, suggests steps to be taken, and identifies mechanisms that will support the change process.
- Culture is a dominant consideration in managing change; steps taken to install new or altered systems trigger cultural reactions. It is essential to integrate systems actions and boundaries with cultural considerations. (The Baldrige Award introduces cultural considerations more specifically than other TQ Trilogy elements; they are, for the most part, mainstream considerations and merit Master Manual tracking.)
- A quality management system is best divided into two phases: launch and operations. Having phases provides an opportunity to gear up for a launch, take the extra steps to ensure success, and learn from limited commitments and activities. The operations phase converts the new or expanded initiative into a normal business operation, applies learning, and may permit throttling back on energy and resources.
- Quality management system launch planning and execution involves a series of steps designed to clarify issues, gain agreement, and achieve commitment. It also involves design of the operations phase(s), definition of communication and training investments, and coordination of follow-up activities. The essential activities cascade downward in the organization.
- The Evergreen component of the introduction and maintenance of new or expanded systems is designed to ensure their longevity and sustainability.
- The Evergreen System is a series of structure and content considerations; it takes the form of a checklist approach to the introduction and maintenance of a new system.
- Creating a quality management system is doable on a self-help basis with conscientious application of job aids and other tools.

Let's look ahead now to Part Two, which presents the TQM Trilogy in detail.

Part Two

Tapping the World's Quality Management Wisdom

A strong case can be made that the Baldrige Award is all you need for an excellent quality management system, especially with the 1991 and 1992 scoring changes in language and weighting. This produced a general tightening in terms of what, where, how, and how much (1991), and added a specific focus on financial and operating results (1992).*

But if we focused exclusively on the Award, what would we miss?

The European Community

First, we would be ignoring some compelling considerations—particularly in relation to European Community initiatives. Although certainly not limited to the EC, the ISO Standards owe their very existence to it. For a while, there were those who predicted that the EC would never gel. Now the original twelve nations of the EC are being besieged by other nations wanting to join the effort.

*As a result of Wallace Co. winning the Award and then going into Chapter 11 bankruptcy.

Organizational leaders cannot ignore the ISO 9000 Standards; then they can consider the Baldrige Award, the logical next step. After all, if I understand the importance of the ISO 9000 process, and potential customers are nipping at my heels to get involved with the Baldrige process, should I not combine my energies and resources and tackle both? The "insistent presence" of the need for ISO 9000 registration simply enhances my interest in the Baldrige process.

Am I being realistic? Yes, I am. How else to account for the fact that the National Institute of Standards and Technology (NIST) distributes about 200,000 copies of the Baldrige *Guidelines* each year, against 100 applications? Where are all these copies going? Why are people even looking at them? The most likely guess is that the ISO 9000 participation requirement for trade facilitation is driving interest in the Baldrige competition option. Early Baldrige Award winners, notably Motorola, Inc., notified existing and potential vendors that to sell into the company, Baldrige participation was a prerequisite— not winning, of course, but *participation*.

The Pacific Rim

Second, we cannot ignore the Pacific Rim—specifically, Japan. We have been eating its dust for years in a number of areas. We exported quality control and quality assurance processes to the Japanese in the early 1950s, and then they beat us at our own game. MADE IN JAPAN has changed from a curse to an accolade. Meanwhile, it is no secret that many U.S. organizations still have waste, scrap, and return rates of a terrifying 20–30 percent. In areas where we both have competing products, the Japanese have (in the aggregate) created and managed quality processes that make our performance pale by comparison. The quality war stories about automobiles and electronics have become legends; the battles being waged to offset or diminish the impact of Japanese quality on worldwide market share have become front-page stories in the United States. Fortunately, there has been some progress.

Europe and Southeast Asia

Third, new quality initiatives are being brought forth in Europe and Southeast Asia. The pressure is becoming relentless; we are surrounded. Does this sound like war? You'd better believe it! That's how the senior quality leaders at the Pentagon talk about our world-wide situation.

Thus, Part Two will circle the globe in terms of the international situation, examine each TQM Trilogy element in detail, and demonstrate how to use the Trilogy to install quality *management* while installing *quality* management. First, however, we have to take an overall look at the TQM Trilogy and evaluate the potential contributions of each component to a quality management system. To put the TQM Trilogy to use, we should be able to pinpoint our strengths and weakness.

How It Works

Generally, the Trilogy builds from the ISO Series, moves on through the Deming Prize, and ends with the Baldrige Award. But the progression is not smooth. The approach in this book will be first to identify twelve major subsystems that constitute an overall quality management system as shown in the box on pages 36–37. The next step will be to evaluate each element of the Trilogy against each of the twelve subsystems, using codes ranging from "no attention" to "great attention." That way, we can draw some conclusions about relative strengths and weaknesses.

Of the twelve subsystems, all are covered by the three Trilogy instruments, but with sizable variations in score.

ISO 9000 Series

- Escalates in detail and complexity from 9001 to 9003.
- Covers all twelve items in model. It is the only instrument that hits item 10 (all four standards).
- On Items 3 and 4, it is as demanding as any other Trilogy instrument; on item 9, it is more demanding.
- Best contributions: documentation and traceability, production process, and testing. Only coverage of packaging and inventory.
- ISO 9004 makes a valuable contribution by adding consideration of management organization and leadership, quality

Trilogy Evaluation Worksheet

	Baldrige	Deming	ISO 9001	ISO 9002	ISO 9003	ISO 9004	Other*
1. Management leadership/ operational performance/ quality procedures/ continuous program elements/wall-to-wall deployment†	1	2	2	2	4	___	___
2. Market research/planning design procedures/ product-service development	0	0	2	2	3	___	___
3. Purchasing-procurement proficiency/contracting methods/supplier performance	0	2	2	0	2	___	___
4. Handling/labeling/ storage/safety	0	1	1	0	1	___	___
5. Documentation/records/ control procedures/ policies/traceability	2	3	3	4	2	___	___
6. Human resources management/training/ development/education	1	1	2	2	4	___	___
7. Transformation and added value (production/service process activities)	0	3	3	4	3	___	___
8. Process quality control/ standards/quality results/ benchmarking/auditing	1	2	2	4	3	___	___
9. Inspection/testing/test equipment/tagging- logging/corrective action/ control of non- conforming output	2	3	3	1	1	___	___
10. Packaging/handling/ inventory procedures	2	2	2	0	0	___	___

	Baldrige	Deming	ISO 9001	ISO 9002	ISO 9003	ISO 9004	Other*
11. Marketing/distribution/ delivery/installation/ operation	0	0	0	0	2	___	___
12. Customer service/ customer satisfaction/ guarantees-warranties	0	0	2	0	4	___	___

Codes:

0 No attention
1 Slight attention
2 Moderate attention
3 Heavy attention
4 Great attention

*"Other" column anticipates additional resources, most likely state-level or professional field processes, which you can evaluate for yourself.

†ISO 9004 contains significant information about system management and administration on a "guideline" basis; many of the key quality concepts are incorporated in the Master Manual strategy used in capturing the best of the TQM Trilogy. ISO 9001-3 is characterized by very specific details around quality techniques and practices. Technically, the Deming Prize can be the broadest source of inspiration because preparation requires *consultation* with the Japanese Union of Scientists and Engineers, the awarding organization. This could be much more far-ranging than the *written* management system and Master Manual guidance in ISO 9004 or the Baldridge Award model. The MBNQA is the most comprehensive model in terms of general management considerations. The written self-help elements of the Deming Prize model reinforce ISO with heavy emphasis on statistical controls.

management procedures, documentation and record keeping, and human resources development and management. It introduces an effective mechanism for organizing the quality effort through a quality manual approach.

Deming Prize

- Covers seven of twelve items in model. Misses totally on items 3, 4, 10, 11, and 12. Uniqueness comes from the very intense coverage of items 5, 7, and 8 (traditional quality program elements).

- On items 7 and 8, it is more demanding than any other Trilogy instrument (all are 4s).
- Always overlaps with other instruments.
- Same as ISO on three items of the seven-item overlap (items 1, 2, and 6); higher on two (items 7 and 8); lower on two (items 1 and 9); tied on one (item 5).
- Same as Baldrige on one item of the same seven-item overlap (item 9); higher on three (items 5, 7, and 8); lower on three (items 1, 2, and 6).
- Best contributions: quality control/assurance organization, documentation, production process, statistical quality control.

Baldrige Award

- Covers eleven of twelve items in model; misses totally on item 10.
- On items 2, 6, 11, and 12, it is more demanding than all the others. On items 3 and 4, it is equally demanding.
- Same as ISO on five items of eleven-item overlap (items 1, 3, 4, 7, and 8); higher on four (items 2, 6, 8, and 12); lower on two (items 5 and 9).
- Same as Deming on one item of seven-item overlap (item 9); higher on three (items 1, 2, and 6); lower on three (items 5, 7, and 8).
- Best contributions: management organization, market research and product development, human resources development and management, production process, process control and quality results, and customer satisfaction.

An Important Caution!

Organizations that have been successful in the quality arena have taken actions to fit their own situations. Struggling companies are well advised to work with rudimentary approaches, such as improved communication and teamwork and reducing costs through quality improvements. Clearly superior companies can tackle the entire spectrum of improvements. *Clearly superior* does not mean huge; it means companies with effective management processes already in place. Unfortunately, it is not unusual in major transformation efforts for the best to get better while the others often stumble and fall.

3

ISO 9000 and International Certification

ISO is the International Organization for Standardization headquartered in Geneva, Switzerland. ISO 9000 is a series of five international standards for quality management. ISO 9000 provides concepts and definitions; ISO 9001, 9002, and 9003 cover specific aspects of a quality assurance program; ISO 9004 gives advice on creating and sustaining a quality management system. The key concept involved in the ISO 9000 Series is its application in trade. Third-party registration agencies certify organizations and locations as having met one of the three specific standards. This creates assurance that the organization can perform according to the quality specifications designated in a contract and should facilitate trade across distance and political boundaries.

A Seal of Approval

Certification or registration is not new. Many household products have a "seal of approval," and electrical appliances are certified as safe by independent laboratories. There are numerous government and industrial standards and certifications. What are new are standards to facilitate trade.

It is easy to understand the current interest in the ISO 9000 Series. Registration under quality standards will almost certainly be necessary if companies are to compete effectively internationally. Virtually all manufacturing organizations will be expected by their customers to be registered under ISO 9001, 9002, or 9003. This is especially important in Europe, where the EC '92 bloc has adopted the ISO concept as the basis for contracting. The rationale is to facilitate trade by simplifying contracting and to obtain related savings with reduced site inspections and audits.

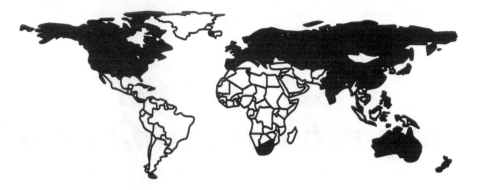

Note: The twelve nations of the European Community have adopted the ISO 9000 Standards as a bloc. In early 1992, the EC and European Free Trade Association (EFTA) announced a combined initiative, the European Economic Area. The pact will bring EFTA into compliance with EC's single-market plan. This adds seven nations. EC 92's functions were effective as of December 31, 1992.

The ISO Series was also adopted, almost word for word, by the United States as the ANSI/ASQC Q90–Q94 series. The American National Standards Institute (ANSI) was founded in 1918 to eliminate conflict and duplication in the voluntary standards development process. ANSI is the U.S. member body of the ISO, which has 91 member countries. Today, ANSI guides the efforts of more than 250 major standards-developing organizations. The American Society for Quality Control (ASQC) is the U.S. contact to ISO through its participation in the ISO committee structure.

The ISO 9000 series is a good starting point for you to create a top-notch management system—one that is excellent in many of the areas necessary for long-lasting performance and profitability. Later, you will want to include the additional dimensions and insights provided by the Deming Prize and the Baldrige Award. Any company that develops a quality system sound enough for registration under ISO 9001 or 9002 will have a leg up on participation in the Baldrige process; ISO registration may even increase Baldrige applications.

There is one major distinction to be made between the elements in the TQM Trilogy: ISO 9000 focuses on the ability to achieve standards negotiated in a contract, and the Deming Prize and Baldrige Award focus on continuous improvement toward achievement of world-class quality levels.

The Registration Process

There are two phases to registration (see Exhibit 3-1 for definitions). The first involves choosing the appropriate Standard, creating a quality system as evidenced by a quality manual (our Master Manual is the management analog), and installing the system as evidenced by achievement of relevant objectives. This chapter concentrates on the first phase.

The second phase entails third-party certification that acknowledges the organization's registered status under ISO 9000. Registration is renewed periodically, depending on the certifying agency involved, but two to three years is the norm between site visits. The second phase is not discussed in detail here, as our purpose is to improve the management process, not to achieve registration.

Selecting an ISO Standard

ISO 9003 is basic; it fits the needs of many smaller, uncomplicated organizations and is a starting point in quality system development. But

Exhibit 3-1. An ISO glossary.

---

accreditation A favorable assessment by the Registrar Accrediting Board (RAB) in the United States or a counterpart in another nation attesting to a registrar's compliance with applicable requirements.

assessment The auditing process in which internal systems, structures, and documentation are examined and reviewed by a registering agency; much of this effort involves checking the ability of employees and associates to execute operating procedures.

certification A favorable assessment by an accredited registrar attesting to a company's compliance with the requirements of a specified quality system (ISO 9001, 9002, or 9003).

registrar An organization engaged in auditing companies that provide products or services to assess their compliance with the standardized requirements of a specified quality system.

Registrar Accreditation Board (RAB) A private, nonprofit organization that ensures the competence of quality systems registrars through accreditation to international standards.

registration A listing of a registrar in a register maintained by RAB or the listing of a supplier of products and services in a register maintained by a registrar.

---

for a full management system as envisioned here, the best choice is ISO 9001. ISO 9002 is an attractive alternative, however, because it is somewhat less comprehensive and thus easier to achieve than registration under 9001. The few differences in ISO 9001 bring it into a broader arena and link it, in a way, to the Baldrige Award.

Here is a brief description of what each Standard covers:

ISO 9000 (Q90):	Road map to the other quality standards in the series; key definitions and principal concepts; the use of quality standards for contractual purposes; assistance in selecting the appropriate Standard
ISO 9001 (Q91):	Quality system model for a contract requiring supplier capability to *design*, produce, inspect, test, train, install, and *service* (the emphasis showing the key additions relative to the following Standard)
ISO 9002 (Q92):	Quality system model for a contract requiring supplier capability to *produce*, inspect, test, train, and *install*
ISO 9003 (Q93):	Quality system model for a contract requiring supplier capability to inspect, test, and train
ISO 9004 (Q94) *(Part 1):*	Quality system and quality management guidelines to develop and implement an effective system
ISO 9004 (Q94) *(Part 2, in preparation):*	Services organization standard, including policy and objectives, system management, human resources, and documentation

Exhibit 3-2 compares the coverage provided by each ISO Standard. Here is a detailed coverage by Standard, starting with ISO 9003, the least demanding:

ISO 9003

1. Steps for creating a quality system (documentation procedures, instructions in setting up the system, steps in implementation)
2. Document control (procedures for controlling access, storing appropriately, distributing properly)
3. Product identification (traceability of materials)
4. Inspection and testing (incoming and in-process steps, final approval, record keeping)

Exhibit 3-2. ISO 9001, 9002, and 9003 coverage.

9001	9002	9003	Coverage
x	x		Management responsibility
x	x	x	Quality system
x	x		Contract review
x			Design control
x	x	x	Document control
x	x		Purchasing
x	x		Purchaser-supplied product
x	x	x	Product identification traceability
x	x		Process control
x	x	x	Inspection and testing
x	x	x	Inspection, measuring, and test equipment
x	x	x	Inspection and test status
x	x	x	Control of nonconforming product
x	x		Corrective action
x	x	x	Handling, storage, packaging, and delivery
x	x	x	Quality records
x	x		Internal quality audits
x	x	x	Training
x			Servicing
x	x	x	Statistical techniques

5. Inspection, measuring, and test equipment (assurance procedures for physical control, security, calibration, maintenance)
6. Inspection and test status (markings and symbols used in process, authority to release results)
7. Control of nonconforming product (prevention of inadvertent use of products that do not pass inspection, documentation of status, disposition)
8. Handling, storage, packaging, and delivery (documentation to track through the several steps, procedures to accomplish it)
9. Quality records (collection of records, indexing, filing, storage)
10. Training process (needs determination, training effectiveness, qualification steps required and accomplished, records)
11. Statistical techniques (procedures for selecting statistics of choice, evaluation of effectiveness of techniques)

ISO 9002

Adds seven significant elements in the two categories of production and installation.

1. Management responsibility (specification of quality policy, the quality organization, verification and validation of quality achievements, and the review process to ensure ongoing quality success)
2. Contract review (procedures for ensuring appropriate agreements)
3. Purchasing (determination of product conformance to requirements, contractor or vendor assessments)
4. Purchase of supplied product (verification that characteristics match requirements, storage and maintenance once products are received)
5. Process control (production/installation processes, monitoring of results)
6. Corrective action (investigations, analyses, prevention controls)
7. Internal quality audits (compliance methods, effectiveness checks of audit activities, follow-up)

ISO 9001

Adds two important categories: designing and servicing.

1. Design control (procedures, planning, coordination of inputs and outputs, verification of correctness in light of requirements)
2. Servicing (procedures for performing service and verifying that requirements were met)

ISO Registration Pluses, Minuses, and Myths

There are clear advantages to ISO registration. It:

- Builds a quality system and provides a foundation for a management system.
- Facilitates trade through assurances of contract performance.
- Provides international recognition and engenders global uniformity.
- Meets European Community business requirements.
- Eliminates (or diminishes) customer audits or surveys.
- Enhances credibility and improves documentation and traceability activities.
- Leads to an organized, written collection of fundamental practices (Master Manual).

There are, however, concerns among quality professionals about potential problems with ISO registration, including:

- Proper accreditation of auditors and registrars
- Consistent administration by registrars
- Consistent interpretation of criteria among registrars
- Possible conflicts of interest among those who provide registration and also consult
- Universal acceptance across *all* industries (it is likely that some industries will supplement the standards)
- Significant direct and overhead costs for the implementation and certification process, including staffing and training
- Minimal attention to statistical quality or process control (which is unthinkable in the Deming Prize process)
- No attention to broad-gauge deployment of quality processes throughout the organization, continuous process improvement, or the ensuring of system longevity

Myths Surrounding ISO 9000

These should not keep an organization from pursuing registration.

- *There is an ISO 9000 requirement to which all companies trading outside their borders must respond.* False: Registration is voluntary; however, customer companies may require registration from their vendors.

- *One must be a specialist in a particular industry to implement the ISO 9000 Series in that industry.* False: The underlying quality control/quality assurance (QC/QA) model is sufficiently generic to fit almost all enterprises. There are qualified professionals and managers in most companies who can handle added ISO requirements. Professionals with a background in organizational development can be particularly helpful in system planning and design; their expertise in managing change can help implementation.

- *The ISO 9000 Series applies primarily to companies that export to Europe (EC '92).* False: The Series applies to the particular situation a company faces in terms of its selling patterns and preferences; for example, both the United States and Canada are signatories to the quality accord. Selling across the border in either direction could prompt interest in the registration process.

- *Every operating procedure must be documented to satisfy ISO 9000 Series registration requirements.* False: Documentation is clearly a hallmark of the ISO process; the ISO requirement focuses only on those elements that are specified in the Standard involved.

• *It is difficult (and costly) to get ISO certification.* False: "Good" companies and experienced QA/QC professionals should have little trouble coping with ISO registration. People costs and consulting fees are tied to the desired level of registration and organizational complexity. Logically, ISO 9003 is the least expensive, since it is the least complicated, and it takes less time to obtain registration under it. Depending on consulting fees and the number of people involved, the two steps—preregistration audit and registration site visit—will cost $15,000–$20,000. The periodic visits—one or two days every year or as agreed upon with the registering agency—will cost $2,500–$3,000. And as more agencies become certified to register companies, transportation expenses should drop.

• *ISO 9000 does not apply to nonmanufacturing organizations.* False: The ISO model can be applied to numerous production operations other than manufacturing; examples include nuclear power generation and petroleum or coal extraction. A version of ISO 9000 for service organizations is under development.

• *There is only one way to achieve registration, and that is through ISO itself.* False: With the help of ASQC, numerous organizations are being chartered to register companies under ISO 9000. There is some controversy, however, about how registration agencies are chosen, potential conflicts of interest, and their longevity as viable financial entities.

ISO 9000 Costs

One of the large costs in implementing a new quality system—which includes publishing a quality manual, surveying the present situation, making adjustments, and altering policies and procedures—is paying for management and professional time. It will probably take one professional four to six months to prepare the paperwork for a preregistration visit. There also is the payroll cost (and time away from other activities) of all the people needed to write and review quality procedures. These activities are a foundation for a broad-gauge quality management system.

In preparing for registration, you must consider the time involved in checking that people can perform prescribed procedures; if they cannot, they must be trained. In fact, the major ISO cost issue for registration will probably be training. First-year training activities may involve 30 to 50 percent of the operating-level work force as well as of most managers, supervisors, and professionals.

Is the ISO 9000 Process Right for You?

Your answers to the following ten questions will help you determine whether the ISO 9000 process is right for your organization:

1. Why consider registration under the ISO 9000 Series?
2. What ISO Standard (e.g., 9001, 9002, or 9003) makes sense at your location?
3. Do all elements of the selected Standard seem to fit?
4. What steps must you take to achieve registration?
5. What can you do with a registration? What are the pluses for your organization?
6. Are there some registration negatives to consider? If so, what? Why?
7. What level of training investment will be needed?
8. How will a program leader be identified and selected?
9. How will you staff for process installation and the assembling of the Master Manual?
10. What budgeting actions do you need to get started?

If you decide that ISO 9000 is a good starting point for your management system, proceed to the following steps:

1. Set up a steering group or task force; initiate a communication effort to create awareness of the quality initiative and the need for it.
2. Select an appropriate Standard and review existing procedures against the Standard requirements in detail. Flowcharts are helpful in visualizing exactly what is going on currently and identifying improvement opportunities.
3. Identify tasks to be accomplished (new, changed approaches).
4. Launch your quality program/process.
5. Define, document, and implement new or revised operating procedures; use flowcharts as appropriate.
6. Compile a Master Manual for management processes and quality initiatives (see the section following and Chapter 6). The fundamental concept, the protocol for change, is a *locally tailored* Master Manual.
7. Develop documentation, tracking, and evaluation procedures (see Chapter 6).
8. Initiate "basic" quality training (e.g., system details, introduction to control).

9. Monitor implementation, check use of procedures, and develop results data.
10. Meet with the assessment organization or agency for a prereg-istration audit; obtain feedback and make adjustments.
11. Develop your final version of the Master Manual and secure needed approvals.
12. Host compliance audit site visit, clear discrepancies.
13. Achieve certification/registration.

ISO 9004

System Master Manual for Management and Quality

The fundamental purposes of your locally tailored Master Manual are as follows:

- To describe the primary focus of your quality management system and the Manual itself; the Manual serves as a permanent guide and reference for your system launch and maintenance
- To communicate philosophy, objectives, and mechanisms for managing your system
- To describe methods for making changes, modifications, revisions, or additions
- To cascade information downward, with the most complete version set up for the top of the organization
- To communicate your strategic and operational quality plans
  —Objectives by level and organizational component
  —Organizational activities and schedule
  —Allocation of responsibilities, authorities by phase (e.g., launch, operational)
  —Specific procedures and channels to be used
  —Locally tailored forms (pages) to be completed to cover all elements of the selected Standard
  —Existing programs to be coordinated (e.g., testing, inspection, audit) by stage (e.g., design, development)
  —Preferred methods for accomplishing system installation (e.g., orientation and training, introducing statistical process control)
- To describe concepts for managing interface issues (e.g., problem solving, allocating resources)
- To educate employees on essential quality approaches at a basic level (depth provided in unit training initiatives)
- To provide supporting documentation, which takes several forms

(by level, such as corporate, division, or group; by supplements that provide specialized technical coverage)

Other Contributions to Your Management System

ISO 9004 also suggests system content beyond that contained in ISO 9001–9003. The sections that are unique and important have to do with issues of system management, documentation, and human resources utilization. This brings the ISO Series closer to the Baldrige Award than the Deming Prize in terms of comprehensiveness. The relevant ISO 9004 content is paraphrased and summarized below.

Management and Leadership Issues

General:
- Highest management levels have responsibility for, and must be committed to, a basic quality management system.
- Management must appropriately resource the system.

Quality Policy:
- Management should announce its corporate quality management policy, which should be consistent with other policies and company values.
- Management should take all appropriate steps to ensure that its quality management approach is communicated, implemented, and sustained over time.

Specific Quality Objectives:
- Management should define objectives for the key elements of quality (e.g., performance, reliability, consistency, value added) in the quality policy. Objectives should be consistent with other corporate objectives and the quality policy.
- Quality costs should always be an important consideration; the objective is to minimize quality losses at an appropriate quality cost level.

Quality System:
- The elements are organizational structure, roles and responsibilities, procedures, and processes and feedback requirements for implementing quality management.
- The quality management system is the means by which stated management and quality policies and objectives are to be accomplished.
- The quality system should be tailored to the particular type of business and the business situation.

- The quality management system, to be in tune with today's approach to quality, should function so as to provide confidence that:
  —It is easily understood and effective.
  —Internal and external customer expectations are satisfied.
  —Prevention is emphasized rather than detection.
- Responsibilities (general, specific), accountabilities, and reporting and communication channels should be explicitly defined.
- Delegation (responsibility, authority) should be clearly established and sufficient to attain assigned objectives with desired efficiency.
- Interface control and coordination measures between different activities should be defined; broadly accepted protocols should be in place for problem resolution and resource distribution disputes.
- Emphasis should be placed on identification of actual or potential problems and the initiation of effective "fixes" or preventive measures.
- Provision must be made for sufficient and appropriate resources (e.g., human resources personnel having specialized skills and experiences; training; inspection, test, and examination equipment; computer hardware and software).

Human Resources Development and Management Issues

Training:
- In general, it is essential to identify quality training needs and provide mechanisms to deliver at all levels and to newly hired and transferred personnel.
- Executive and management personnel must:
  —Understand the quality management system.
  —Have tools and techniques to operate the quality system.
  —Accept and use evaluation criteria for system effectiveness.
- Professional and technical personnel must:
  —Have broad-gauge training to enhance their management system contribution (see Appendix B).
  —Be trained in statistical techniques at appropriate levels of complexity.
- Production supervisors and workers must have:
  —Methods and skills to perform tasks (e.g., operation of instruments, tools, and machinery; reading and understanding documentation; relationship of work to quality objectives; safe operations)

   —Training in basic statistical techniques, as needed
   —Operator certification, as appropriate

Performance Management:
- *Orientation and awareness:*
  —Create understanding of tasks expected to be performed and their relationship to overall quality activities.
  —Establish the necessity for proper job performance at *all* levels.
  —Clarify how poor job performance affects other employees, customer satisfaction, operating costs, and the organization's profitability.
- *Certification.* Establish a competency-based system tied to recognition and rewards.
- *Application.* Efforts should cover all who can impact quality, both by assignment and by level.
- *Feedback.* Everyone involved must know how things are going, individually and organizationally.

Quality Measurement:
- Publicize definitive measures of quality achievement by individuals and teams to validate the system and encourage continuing creation of appropriate quality.
- Recognize performance when satisfactory quality levels are attained.

Registration Agencies

ASQC is the central contact point for information about registration sources in the United States. Its wholly owned, not-for-profit subsidiary, the Registrar Accreditation Board (RAB), accredits agencies against a set of standards and publishes a directory. RAB has recognized a number of U.S. agencies that can conduct independent, third-party, on-site audits and provide registration. Registration by one of these agencies may be publicized. Periodic recertification time frames and reaudit practices vary.

    Some U.S. companies trading into EC '92 opt for a European certification source on the basis of enhanced credibility in the market area. At the time of publication, Underwriters' Laboratories was the largest and most familiar U.S. organization registering under the ISO 9000 Series.

You can order the ANSI/ASQC version of the ISO 9000 Series from:

American Society for Quality Control
310 W. Wisconsin Ave.
Milwaukee, WI 53203
(414) 272–8575
(800) 248–1746 (fax: 414-272-1734) for placing orders

A complete set of materials costs under $50 (plus postage and handling). To pursue the steps recommended here, you will need only ISO 9000, 9001, and 9004; they may be available as a special package at a lower price. Major credit cards are accepted, and there is a discount for ASQC members.

Actions to Consider

- Determine how many parts of your organization will need a Master Manual.
- Obtain three-ring binders.
- Design your Master Manual Tracking Sheet (see Chapter 6).
- Go through ISO 9001 and 9004 for relevant (against your mission and objectives) dimensions. Create a tracking sheet(s) for each one. Note that your different organizational elements will have both core and exclusive dimensions to track. Production operations will have the most; small administrative groups will have the least. Additional Trilogy elements will add dimensions to track; the Baldrige will have the greatest impact on nonproduction groups.

4

The Deming Prize and Statistical Control

The following equates ISO 9000 with the Deming Prize.

Contrast of ISO 9000 Registration and the Deming Prize Competition

	ISO 9000	*Deming*
Purpose	"Effectively document the Quality System elements to be implemented or in place needed to ensure an ability to perform; voluntary registration by an accredited third party."	"Award prizes to those companies recognized as having applied CWQC (Company-Wide Quality Control) based on Statistical Quality Control." Emphasizes "world-class" accomplishments.
Emphasis	Validation of ability to perform according to contract.	Statistical process control.
Eligibility	Companies, divisions, locations in countries signatory to the ISO protocol (includes U.S., Canada).	Individuals, factories, and companies— global since 1984; only non-Japanese winner has been Florida Power and Light.

(continues)

53

	ISO 9000	*Deming*
Participants	Typically, organizations involved in international trade that wish to be acceptable as vendors, especially those wishing to trade with EC '92.	Any number of companies that meet the standard established by the Union of Japanese Scientists and Engineers (JUSE).
Evaluation Criteria	ISO 9001/Q91: Definitions. ISO 9001–3; Q91–93: Standards at three levels of depth and breadth. ISO 9004/Q94: Guidelines.	One page of guidelines ("Particulars")—very succinct, with some subjective interpretation (JUSE personnel judgments).
Orientation	Process (80 percent) at 9001 level; heavy on quality assurance initiatives; management and administration (20 percent).	Process (60 percent) plus results (40 percent); heavy on statistical process control.
Mechanics	Select registration agency; pre-assessment choice of standard, submission of quality Master Manual, site assistance visit; on-site assessment of three to five days.	Qualification based on review off-/on-site by JUSE.
Examiners	Select staff of registration agency; ASQC maintains a list of recommended registrars; some companies prefer to use an EC '92 source.	Select panel of senior members of JUSE.

	ISO 9000	Deming
Cost	Low to moderate dollars with sound quality assurance program in place; some consulting on system may be useful.	High dollars and effort; consulting fees from JUSE are a major component (training has a major impact in any case).
Time Frame	Registration takes six to twelve months depending on starting point and urgency.	Two to five years (preparation with JUSE; application when "ready").
Common Emphases	Administration, procedures, controls, training.	

The Deming Prize was instituted in 1951 by the Union of Japanese Scientists and Engineers (JUSE) in recognition of Dr. W. Edwards Deming's friendship and achievements in the cause of industrial quality control (QC). Deming was invited to Japan in 1950 to present a series of lectures as part of quality seminars organized by JUSE. His contributions provided a vital stimulus to early efforts to use industrial quality control in Japan, which was still occupied by the U.S. military, and there were a number of initiatives to import U.S. technology and administrative approaches. It is now management folklore that Japan took what we had, converted it to its best use in Japan, and is reexporting the results to the United States.

Deming's impact was pervasive. QC was adopted in virtually every sector of Japanese industry and evolved over time into the concept of total or companywide quality control. The impact abroad has been significant, especially in the United States, where total quality control was a formative element in the creation of the Baldrige Award.

It has become customary for Japanese corporations wishing to improve their performance in products or services to vie for the Deming Prize to benefit not only from the prestige that goes with the honor but also from the internal improvements that result from the required implementation of total quality control.

Deming Prize Categories

There are two broad categories of Deming Prize: the Individual Person and the Application Prize. The Application Prize has four subcategories:

Overall Organization, Overseas Company, Division, and Small Enterprise. There is also a Quality Control for Factory Prize.

Judging

The Deming Prize Committee is responsible for selecting those individuals and organizations to be recognized. It is chaired by the chairman of the board of directors of JUSE or a person recommended by the board. The Committee is made up of members chosen by the chairman from among those with knowledge and experience and officers of organizations related to quality control. The Application Prize Subcommittee is made up of university professors and quality control experts in government and other nonprofit institutions. The Committee reviews applications, performs on-site examinations, and awards prizes. In the first 38 years of the Deming Prize process, there have been 138 Japanese winners (see Exhibit 4-1 for the number of winners in each category).

Prize Application and Selection Process

It is generally understood that JUSE consultants work with companies to prepare them through a quality control diagnosis. Prize application is made in the year following the one in which the JUSE consultants finish their work. An application form must be completed by November 20, and a preliminary decision on whether technical eligibility requirements as to prize category are met is made by December 20.

Upon notification of acceptance, the applicant submits a Description

Exhibit 4-1.   Deming Prize winners in each category (1951–1989).

Prize	Number
Application Prize (Overall)	88*
Application Prize for Small Enterprise	32
Application Prize for Division	5
Application Prize for Overseas Company	1**
Quality Control for Factory	13
Total	139

*Two U.S. companies (Texas Instruments and Xerox) have been part owners of Japanese companies that have won the Deming Prize.
**Florida Power and Light.

of QC Practices and a company business prospectus, both written in Japanese, no later than January 20. If the Description is approved, the applicant's on-site examination occurs sometime between March 20 and September 30. Prizewinners are selected between October 10 and October 20, and the prize ceremony is held in November. Exhibit 4-2 summarizes the mechanics of the Deming Prize application process.

Quality Criteria

The conditions under which quality control (assurance) must be implemented are specifically defined in the Deming Prize Checklist (see Exhibit 4-3). The Description should include the progress made in QC

(Text continues on page 60)

Exhibit 4-2. The mechanics of Deming Prize application.

There is a maximum number of pages the Description should contain, depending on the number of employees in an organization:

Under100:	50
Under 2,000:	75
For each additional	
*500 over 2,000:**	5

On-site inspection can involve any group from the CEO's staff to the smallest unit (but not under ten employees); sampling may be employed if it is deemed necessary.** There are two to six examiners per unit. The passing grade is on average 70 percent at all levels; a score of less than 50 percent for any unit will cause the organization to fail. There are provisions for follow-up inspections if a qualifying grade is not achieved on the first try.

The length of on-site visits is two to three days for all levels down to the branch, sales office, and laboratory levels; then the commitment drops to one to two days.

Application costs include the current per diem for each examiner—$810 to $1,215 per day (portal to portal)—first-class air fare, first-class hotel accommodations (single room with bath), three meals daily, miscellaneous expenses, cost of preparing a written opinion, and interpreter or translator fees.

---

* The Baldrige application is limited to seventy-five pages, with provision for additional pages for major divisions.

** The theory of probability is often used, but there are also numerous formulas and charts to help determine randomness and size. Such a determination is one of the most technical issues in traditional quality control statistics and goes to the design of an experiment.

Exhibit 4-3. Deming Prize checklist.

---

1. *Policies.* How are policies determined and transmitted? What results have been achieved?

   • Policies pursued for management, quality, and quality control
   • Method of establishing policies
   • Justifiability and consistency of policies
   • Utilization of statistical methods
   • Transmission and diffusion of policies
   • Review of policies and the results achieved
   • Relationship between policies and long- and short-term planning

2. *Organization and its management.* How are scopes of responsibility and authority defined? How is cooperation promoted and quality control managed?

   • Explicitness of the scopes of authority and responsibility
   • Appropriateness of delegations of authority
   • Interdivisional cooperation
   • Committees and their activities
   • Utilization of staff
   • Utilization of QC circle activities
   • Quality control diagnosis

3. *Education and dissemination.* How is quality control taught, and how is training delivered to employees? To what extent are QC and statistical techniques understood? How are QC circle activities utilized?

   • Education programs and results
   • Quality- and control-consciousness and degree of understanding of quality control
   • Teaching of statistical concepts and methods and the extent of their dissemination
   • Grasp of the effectiveness of quality control
   • Education of related companies (particularly those in the same group, subcontractors, consignees, and distributors)
   • QC circle activities
   • System for suggesting improvements

4. *Collection, dissemination, and use of information on quality.* How is information collected and disseminated at various locations inside and outside the company? How well is it used? How quickly?

   • Collection of external information
   • Transmission of information between divisions
   • Speed of information transmission (use of computers)

  • Data processing, statistical analysis of information, and utilization of results

5. *Analysis.* Are critical problems grasped and analyzed against overall quality and the production process? Are they interpreted appropriately, using the correct statistical methods?

  • Selection of key problems and themes
  • Propriety of analytical research
  • Utilization of statistical methods
  • Linkage with proper technology
  • Quality analysis, process analysis
  • Utilization of analytical results
  • Assertiveness of improvement suggestions

6. *Standardization.* How are standards used, controlled, and systematized? What is their role in enhancement of company technology?

  • Systematization of standards
  • Method of establishing, revising, and abolishing standards
  • Outcome of the establishment, revision, or abolition of standards
  • Content of the standards
  • Utilization of statistical methods
  • Accumulation of technology
  • Utilization of standards

7. *Control.* Are quality procedures reviewed for maintenance and improvement? Are responsibility and authority scrutinized, control charts and statistical techniques checked?

  • Systems for the control of quality and such related matters as cost and quantity
  • Control items and control points
  • Utilization of such statistical control methods as control charts and other statistical concepts
  • Contribution to performance of QC circle activities
  • Actual conditions of control activities
  • State of matters under control

8. *Quality Assurance.* Are all elements of the production operation that are essential for quality and reliability (from product development to service) examined, along with the quality assurance management system?

  • Procedures for the development of new products and services (analysis and upgrading of quality, checking of design, reliability, and other properties)

(continues)

Exhibit 4-3. Continued.

- Safety and immunity from product liability
- Process design, process analysis, and process control and improvement
- Process capability
- Instrumentation, gauging, testing, and inspecting
- Equipment maintenance and control of subcontracting, purchasing, and services
- Quality assurance system and its audit
- Utilization of statistical methods
- Evaluation and audit of quality
- Actual state of quality assurance

9. *Effects (results).* Are products of sufficiently good quality being sold? Have there been improvements in quality, quantity, and cost? Has the whole company been improved in quality, profit, scientific way of thinking, and will to work?

- Measurement of results
- Substantive results in such matters as quality, services, delivery, time, cost, profits, safety, and environment
- Intangible results
- Measures for overcoming defects

10. *Future plans.* Are strong and weak points in the present situation recognized? Is promotion of quality control planned and likely to continue?

- Grasp of the present state of affairs and concreteness of the plan
- Measures for overcoming defects
- Plans for further advances
- Linkage with long-term plans

Note: *Quality control* means companywide quality control based on statistical quality control techniques. The Deming Prize model (items and particulars) is basically similar to the ISO 9000 model in that both emphasize quality control/quality assurance. They differ from the Baldrige model in that Baldrige presents a broad-gauge management system. Watch for the differences.

activities, along with features of quality activities that receive high priority. The quality level of main products (compared with the competition) is reported, together with user reactions to tangible and intangible quality results. Aspects of QC that have not been fully achieved are identified, along with plans for improving them. In particular, the relationships across functions and departments are clarified and explained how responsibilities are allocated and collaborative coordination maintained in such areas as new-product development, quality assurance, volumetric control, and cost control.

Deming officials can, and do, consider the following as well:

- Profits
- Cost controls
- Research
- Product development and design
- Equipment maintenance
- Instrumentation and inspection
- Manufacturing processes
- Inventories
- Safety

- Personnel and labor relations
- Delivery performance
- Education and training
- Quality assurance coordination
- Complaint handling
- Customer opinion utilization
- After-sale service
- Relationships (associates, subcontractors, suppliers, customer companies)

With a companywide orientation, the overall operation is scrutinized carefully. Judgments and recommendations are developed through the preparatory consulting contacts, where there may be some subjectivity. However, the Deming Prize Checklist is an orderly way to examine how a company operates. Used in conjunction with the site visit, it provides a comprehensive model that can enhance your local master quality management model. Unlike the ISO 9000 model, it is scored by the examiners, with percentages awarded for each item—70 percent being "passing." Unlike the Baldrige Award, there are no specified weights per item.

You will want to comb through the items and particulars of the Deming Checklist, as you did with the selected ISO 9000 Standard, to determine which elements will add value to your Master Manual. Note the attention to statistics in items 1, 4, 5, 6, 7, and 8, whose particulars focus on statistical applications. Carefully examine items 5, 7, and 8; these particulars go somewhat beyond the ISO Series in establishing a quality management system. Items 2, 3, and 7 introduce the QC circle concept (this is a major addition that is covered in more detail later in this chapter). Make notes as you go.

Specific Actions to Take

1. Go through the items and particulars to select dimensions not covered in ISO 9000 that will assist in creating your quality management system. One example would be the QC circle concept. Criteria for selection of an item for your management system continue to be mission and objectives.

2. Go through the items and particulars that overlap ISO 9000 dimensions in some way and that may strengthen your system; analyze the content and tighten the language.
3. Make the appropriate entries on your Master Manual tracking sheets, by organization.

The Role of Quality Control Circles

Generally attributed to the work of Kaoru Ishikawa (and reported upon by Dr. Joseph M. Juran), quality control (QC) circles are small groups of supervisors and employees who meet to identify, analyze, and solve problems. The QC circle concept immigrated to the United States naturally, since many U.S. companies already employed organizational development technologies and were expert at getting groups together to plan and problem-solve. The general conviction is that problems are solved best by those closest to them, and the involvement is highly motivating.

The logistics vary. Typically, participation is voluntary; meetings may be on or off company time. In one form of QC circle, the participants are given the opportunity to work on a problem identified by management or the quality system; in another form, the circle uses its experience to identify problems that need solution and volunteers to tackle them. In Japan, the usual model is a group within each department that meets at least once a month to study ways of improving quality. Management provides the necessary training, including, in the areas of circle participation, problem analysis, control methodology, and statistics.

In the rush to achieve quality in the United States, the QC circle approach has been tried by some companies without much, if any, preparation or training. That has led to disappointment. Other companies reportedly have hundreds of carefully set-up QC circles and are pleased with their contributions. It is clear that many variations on the basic theme are possible; it is equally clear that the volunteers will expect their ideas and solutions to be respected.

Some companies use the "QC circle" identifier; many choose to develop their own labels. It is common for U.S. companies to want an exclusive approach, even if it is in name only. Anytime a term becomes a buzzword, the concept it describes is susceptible to a new label. Always look at the underlying process in evaluating whether something will work for your company.

The concept of *involvement* applied with the creation of QC circles means nothing more than solicitation of input. Another term associated with the Baldrige Award is very different: *Empowerment* means that individuals, teams, or task forces can take action, with authority delegated to do so.

Statistical Quality Control

The quality movement has focused on metrics: measures that help in understanding markets, processes, results, and customer satisfaction. In some cases, new, expanded, or enhanced measures have made the entire difference in quality improvements. It is easy to forecast that more attention will be paid to measurements involving employee or associate input using survey-feedback technology, but all the applications use statistics of one kind or another.

Measurement Considerations

Statistics help quality. Generally, the same old statistics are used, but with a large dose of enthusiasm added. Today's astonishing situation is a seemingly general acceptance that more measurement means more quality. Everyone measures something, but not everyone needs the same level of detail or skill, and some may not need to measure at all. A recent study commissioned by the General Accounting Office indicates that a quality initiative may have a 70 percent impact on an operations group but only a 10 percent impact on an administrative group.

Exhibit 4-4 presents a basic quality control/assurance program with traditional statistical quality control (SQC) components, but there are other options and alternatives. Choices have to be made so that the measurement and the statistical processes fit the situation and the organizational objectives. New entrants from the behavioral sciences round out today's quality management systems. Exhibit 4-5 presents an overview of available options.

Individual Involvement

Self-measurement is motivating and reinforcing. It makes sense to ask operators and doers of any kind to get involved in measuring what is important in their particular roles. Tracking is involving; being able to take action to improve is empowering, but this may take training.

The statistical requirement may be simply to record or plot numbers. Training people beyond the necessary level is wasteful, and measuring what should not be measured is self-deceptive. People are prac-

Exhibit 4-4. Rudiments of statistical quality control.

Use the following steps to help establish the needed range and depth of investment in SQC in your organization. Keep in mind criteria that will ensure the best decision, such as validity, reliability, reasonable cost, practicality, acceptability, comparability, lasting value, and ability to make a point.

1. Establish the problem or opportunity. What needs controlling?
2. Develop and study a flowchart or "fishbone" diagram to determine locations and/or causes of problems, and decide what steps must be taken.
3. Describe the data to collect:

    • *Scope*—Boundaries that define start/stop, population, time period
    • *Parameters to measure*—Attributes to count, variables to measure, where in the process, types of data, appropriate and useful ratios
    • *Collection mechanics*—Who—operators, specialists, supervisors; how; sampling procedure; costs
    • *Analytical components:*

        —Statistics: average(s), totals, control limits/percentages
        —Frequencies: daily (attribute), monthly (quality characteristic)
        —Comparisons: item types, shift-to-shift
        —Means of reporting: attribute—weekly types, totals; quality characteristic—monthly average, totals
        —Basic charts/graphs: pie, bar, line charts, and sampling tables; scatter diagram (amount of correlation—alleged cause, known effect); histogram (variability within a process; comparison of actual with expected); run chart (stability; plot data in sequence; plot average at twenty points; seven consecutive points on one side indicates out of control); Pareto analysis (prioritize problem areas by severity or importance; applies the "80-20" rule); fishbone chart diagram (cause and effect relationships)

4. Select control chart(s) configuration:

    • *Variables tracking.* Plot specific measurements of a variable, such as size or weight; configurations all have a center line and upper/lower control limits; typically use two (*x-Bar* and *R*) charts that are combined into an *x-Bar-R.*
        —Disadvantage: Many variables mean many charts.
        —Control limits: These are commonly three standard deviations/sigma (99.7 percent). Some world-class targets are Six Sigma.
        —Process average: Use *x-Bar* chart (average/mean calculated and

charted); R chart (range is charted); or a combination x-*Bar-R* (both are plotted, usually with the range on the lower scale; gives specific clues to help isolate a problem.

—Process Variation: Take large sample (ten or more observations per sample); use x-*Bar* and s (standard deviation, sigma) charts. Take small sample (fewer than ten observations possible per sample), average the measurements, take 20 for 100 observations, and use x-*Bar* and R chart for efficiency.

- *Attributes tracking.* Provides summaries of go/no-go situations, such as in or out of tolerance, working or not working; choose between units and number (latter is more precise).

  —Units defective: if n = constant, use p chart (percentage defective) or more commonly, the np chart (number defective); if n = variable, use p chart with control limits (CL) determined by sample size and apply standard formula.

  —Number of defects: If n = constant, use c chart (number of defects per sample) or less commonly, u chart (number of defects per unit); if n = variable, use u chart (number of defects per unit).

---

tical about how they use their time, so measurement for its own sake will not fly.

One key to ponder: Some sophisticated number-crunching has been going on for years; talent and experience are already present in most organizations that benefit from SQC, although very few people may actually be employed to do this kind of work. The new quality "order" probably requires more involvement—it certainly does in the Baldrige process—which may mean anything from a brief orientation on filling out paper-and-pencil records to a light touch of statistical training to a full-blown investment in major training. It may also mean buying or designing new software for personal computers, with an accompanying training requirement.

Improper Handling of Data

There are some things you *don't* want to have happen with your statistics. For example:

- Data fabrication
- Data falsification ("cooking" or altering data)
- Undisclosed conflicts of organizational or professional interest

Exhibit 4-5.   Behavioral science statistics and options.

Statistical quality control is being enhanced by behavioral science statistics as the Baldrige model joins the quality process. One relevant example is the major focus on customer satisfaction. Other statistics are appropriate for customer measurements.

   Presented here is an overview of the processes and techniques involved. You will want to have this capability.

- Organize the measurement activity. This requires definition of issues, data collection, data analysis, and interpretation.
- Use models to introduce nontraditional behavioral science techniques vis-à-vis traditional QA/QC (examples include market research, forecasting, organizational surveys, and customer satisfaction studies). Although generally well-known, they may be a new configuration and mandate a new set of skills in some organizations.
- Know design of study (experimental, ex post facto, descriptive).
- Know probability and variation (distributions, standard error, parametric and nonparametric relationships).
- Know measurement methods and sampling strategies (e.g.: pilots, testing, randomization).
- Know processes fundamental to statistical procedures:

   —Data classification (nominal, ordinal, interval, ratio)
   —Mean, median, mode
   —Standard deviation
   —Range
   —Frequency distribution/cumulative sum techniques
   —Scatter diagram/correlation coefficient
   —Significance testing
   —Regression analysis/analysis of variance (dependent, independent determination)
   —Factor analysis, other multivariate techniques

- Know problem solving as a result of analysis.

- Release of confidential/privileged information
- Irresponsible/incomplete credit given to contributors (such as individuals or groups)
- Sloppy recording of data or failure to retain primary data
- Selective reporting of project/task force findings
- Inappropriate statistical tests and procedures
- Fragmentary, insufficient, or misleading reporting

Considering the Implications of SQC

The following ten questions will help you assess the implications of SQC and other statistical techniques for your organization:

1. What is going to be measured and tracked across the organization? To what purpose? Who will determine what should be done? Are you properly staffed to use SQC and its variations?
2. How will operations be measured and controlled? What are the statistics of choice? Why?
3. What steps are needed to add in behavioral statistics, if relevant? How will new statistics be integrated with traditional ones?
4. What training is needed to provide an appropriate level of understanding of statistics? Will this vary by job? How so? How will it be handled?
5. Are there relevant and useful statistics available with respect to nonproduction operations (e.g., training, accounting, purchasing)?
6. Who will convert measurements to data for analysis and response? Where will data be stored? How will the data be controlled? Are there security considerations (e.g., access)?
7. How can your organization distinguish between the "vital few" measures and the "trivial many"?
8. Will data be shared internally and externally? If either, why? If not, why not? How will this be managed?
9. Is there a standard way to represent and interpret data in your organization? Should there be? How would it work? If not, what can be done to reduce confusion from multiple approaches?
10. Is your organization familiar with computer programs available for SQC? Are any in place? How are they working? Is it time for upgrading?

Significant Quality Leaders

There is a thirty- to forty-year history of discovery and new applications of mathematical approaches to quality assurance and improvement involving approaches similar to those developed by W. Edwards Deming. The leaders were Americans until the statistical processes reached Japan; the Japanese have now made significant contributions of their own. Here is a short list of today's best- known contributors (and the contributions for which they are known) in alphabetical order:

Phillip M. Crosby:	"quality is free" and "zero defects"
W. Edwards Deming, Ph.D.:	"fourteen points" and "seven diseases"
Armand V. Feigenbaum, Ph.D.:	"total quality" (involvement) and "quality costs"
Kaoru Ishikawa:	"quality circles" and "fishbone" problem analysis
Joseph M. Juran, Ph.D.:	"fitness for use" and "Juran Trilogy"

These five quality scientists took the lead in advocating new approaches to quality and provided direction to SQC development or enhancement through their individual genius. The common thread among them is a respect, if not a driving desire, for the use of measurement approaches. Each has had a significant impact on the value attached to and the recent use made of quality technology.

You may find it useful to track down their publications (see the Bibliography) in order to benefit from their philosophies, experiences, and recommendations. Generally speaking, they have not argued for an integrated management system as complete as the one today's executives need, given our challenging economic, demographic, educational, and legal environment.

These five are certainly not alone in their leadership role, but they are prominent and well worth checking out before going into a custom system design.

One caveat must be offered when one sifts through anyone's strongly held positions for inspiration or assistance: Only initiatives that have been custom-tailored for a particular organization and situation seem to work and stay Evergreen over the long run.

Assessing the Suitability of the Deming Prize Model for Your Organization

1. To what extent is your operation one that will benefit from intense application of SQC?
2. What level of intensity of application of SQC is presently in place?
3. What changes to your present SQC operation are suggested by the Deming Prize model? How should they be handled?
4. Is the talent present to handle changes that appear useful?
5. Which of the broader "particulars" seem to offer considerations that you should incorporate in your Master Manual?
6. Can you identify useful applications of the Deming Prize Particulars in organizational elements outside your production operations? If so, what are they?

7. Does the focus on SQC and production operations affect the usefulness of the Deming model for your creation of a Master Manual? Does it advance what you have from ISO 9000?
8. The Deming on-site evaluation also examines such broad considerations as personnel and labor relations, opinions of customers, and after-sale services. Does this alter your view of the usefulness of the Deming Prize Checklist as a model?
9. If the Deming Prize model or details could be improved, what would help you apply its wisdom and experience in your organization?
10. Is there a reason for your organization to consider applying for the Deming Prize? If so, why? If not, why not?

At various public presentations at which Florida Power and Light (FPL) has shared its Deming Prizewinning experience, ten problem points have emerged that are well worth considering as you set up your own system. Some of these effects are contrary to what used to be generally accepted goals for quality management programs in the United States (e.g., less recognition, insensitivity to employee input, bloated bureaucracy).

1. Preoccupation with process, leading to loss of sensitivity to employees and practices such as less recognition for good business decisions than for following quality procedures
2. Management intensity about the challenge of doing what is expected, so that it ignored employee input or was unreceptive when it was volunteered (nothing more than "traditional" supervision)
3. Creation of a formidable bureaucracy for system installation and maintenance and an overemphasis on mechanics
4. Questionable use of people and money ($885,000 in JUSE consulting fees and $400,000 in direct costs were disallowed by the state of Florida for pass-along to consumers)*
5. Counterproductive review processes; inappropriate accountability practices
6. Quality training program investments that were out of balance, favoring mechanics rather than the organization's overall quality competency needs and the level of quality competencies needed by those at or near the front line
7. Expensive "prepping" of employees so that they could respond

---

*It has been reported that FPL's customer complaint rating remained unchanged.

   effectively to on-site assessments, which raised questions
   among employees
 8. Well-intended training and development investments—to
    achieve "lockstep" procedures and a common vocabulary—that
    were not fully effective
 9. Excessive pursuit of metrics and "numbers" and inappropriate
    use of quotas
10. Trouble starting at the beginning, not after the Prize was won.
    There was no Evergreen strategy built into the system to ensure
    future progress and avoid recidivism

For a brochure on the Deming Prize for Overseas Companies and
additional information, contact:

The Deming Prize Committee
Union of Japanese Scientists and Engineers
5-10-11 Sendagaya, Shibuya-ku
Tokyo 151
Japan
(011) 03-5379-1227, 1232 (fax: 03-3225-1813)

5

The Baldrige Award and Management Excellence

The following equates the Deming Prize with the Malcolm Baldrige National Quality Award.

	Deming	*Baldrige*
Contrast of the Deming Prize and the Malcolm Baldrige National Quality Award		
Purpose	Award prizes to those companies recognized as having applied CWQC (Company-wide Quality Control) based on Statistical Quality Control.	Promote quality awareness, recognize quality achievements of U.S. companies, and publicize successful quality strategies.
Emphasis	Statistical methods; prevention of quality problems.	Customer satisfaction; prevention of quality problems.
Eligibility	Individuals, factories, and companies— global since 1984.	Companies only— limited to U.S.

(continues)

	Deming	*Baldrige*
Award Recipients	Any number of companies that meet the standard established by the Union of Japanese Scientists and Engineers (JUSE).	Maximum of two manufacturing companies (plus their divisions), two small companies (less than 500 employees), and two service companies.
Evaluation Criteria	One page of guidelines ("Particulars")—very succinct, broad, subjective interpretation.	Twenty-five pages of guidelines ("Areas to Address, Scoring System, Business Factors Considered")— 1992 issue.
Orientation	Process (60 percent) plus results (40 percent); heavy statistical process control.	Results (60 percent) plus process (40 percent); heavy quality results, customer satisfaction, human resources orientation.
Process	Qualification based on review with JUSE.	Qualification for site visit; competition.
Examiners	Select panel.	Open examiner system; annual application, selection; assignment avoids conflict of interest.
Cost	High dollars and effort; consulting fees from JUSE are a major component (training has a major impact in any case).	Low to high dollars; high effort if excellent quality system(s) not in place (training has a major impact in any case).
Time Frame	Two to five years (preparation with JUSE; application when "ready.")	One-year cycles; renew after five years.

The Malcolm Baldrige National Quality Award Guidelines have become one of the most popular pieces of reading material in American business. In the past few years, around 200,000 copies have been distributed annually, but only 100 or so completed applications have been submitted each year. Add the number of photocopies and privately printed copies and you have an avalanche of copies being used as an organizational tool. What more is there to say about popularity?

Our interest is not in the Award's competition process, although we do review it (see Exhibits 5-1 and 5-2). Our goal is to use the Baldrige model as we have ISO 9000 and the Deming Prize: as an accepted, rational way to manage an enterprise. Unlike the other TQM Trilogy models, the Baldrige Award is scorable; it allows for the distribution of 1,000 points over its examination categories and items. The Baldrige model has improved with experience; it offers a number of important new dimensions that are absolutely essential for a broad management process.

Major Quality System Dimensions for Consideration

• *Approach.* Methods the organization uses to achieve the purposes addressed in the examination items. The considerations are appropriateness and effectiveness of methods, tools, and techniques; degree to which they are prevention-based; degree to which they are systemic, integrated, and consistently applied; use of effective quantitative measures; and incorporation of evaluation and improvement cycles.

• *Deployment.* Extent to which the approaches are applied to all relevant areas and activities addressed and implied in the examination items. The considerations are appropriate and apply effectively to all product or service categories; to all interactions with customers, suppliers, and the public; and to all internal processes, activities, facilities, and employees.

• *Results.* Outcomes and effects in achieving the purposes addressed and implied in the examination items. The considerations include the quality levels demonstrated; contributions of outcomes and effects to quality improvement; rate and breadth of quality improvement; demonstration of sustained improvement; significance of improvements to organization's mission and purposes; comparison with industry and world leaders; and ability to show that improvements derive from quality practices and actions.

Consistent with the philosophy of continuous improvement, the Guidelines change from year to year. On the one hand, this is admirable and useful; on the other hand, it disrupts previously prepared programs

Exhibit 5-1. The mechanics of the Baldrige Award.

Award Goals

- To promote awareness of quality as an increasingly important element in competitiveness
- To enhance understanding of the requirements for quality excellence
- To encourage sharing of information on successful quality strategies and the benefits derived from their implementation.

Award Eligibility

- The three award categories are manufacturing, service, and small businesses.
- Up to two awards may be given in each category each year. (The six available awards have not yet been given in any one year.) Because of the demanding nature of today's model it would be tough for a very large and complex organization to win. Recently, small (or relatively small) manufacturing companies have been most successful in the competition.

Award Publicity and Commitments

- Recipients may publicize and advertise their awards—considered a major plus.
- Recipients are expected to share information about their successful quality strategies with other U.S. organizations.
- In some cases, companies yielded to the temptation to spend too much time and failed to mind the store.

Award Applications

- Companies submit applications that lead to an examination review, based on quality excellence criteria in the Guidelines.
- Each applicant is expected to provide information and data on the company's quality processes and quality improvement. There is a strong emphasis on demonstrated progress; which means tracking data over time. Organizations in good shape to begin with do this routinely and can get ready for the MBNQA competition in short order; others have to set up new systems and track their operation over two or three years to be in a position to compete.

Exhibit 5-2. Baldrige Award scoring.

Percentage of Total Score	0%	50%	100%
Documentation	Anecdotal	Available	Organized, published
Preventive System	Anecdotal	Sound, systematic	Sound, systematic, refined by evaluation
Integration Across Organization	None	Some	Excellent
Major Area Involvement	Anecdotal	Most	All
Support Area Involvement	Anecdotal	Some	All
Longevity	None	Some history (most major areas)	Sustained (all areas); improvement cycles
Results	Anecdotal	Major areas: positive trends	Major areas: world-class; support areas: good to excellent
Evaluation	None	Some evidence that results caused by approach	Clear evidence that results caused by approach

and materials. In the past, the changes have involved both language and scoring weights. Although basic concepts remain in place and allow for some tracking of improvement in the basic management process, the percentage of changes in category and item scoring and wording can run over 80 percent, depending on how they are calculated.

In 1991, the changes involved tightening of the quality of information required. Items called for greater specificity in describing methods, processes, and results; there was more use of terms such as *what* and *how* and *describe*. In 1992, the changes focused on overall company performance and operational results; in addition to strengthening themes such as productivity, work process simplification, and cycle time reduction, there was an important added discussion of the pivotal role of quality and operational results. All in all, these changes clearly improved the Baldrige Award model as a general management tool.

Application Procedures

All Baldrige Award applications are reviewed and evaluated by the five-member board of examiners. When board members are assigned to review applications, their business and quality expertise is matched to the business of the applicant. Strict rules regarding real and potential conflicts of interest are followed in assigning board members to review applications.

Although the National Institute of Standards and Technology of the Department of Commerce governs the Baldrige Award, the applications review process is not funded by the U.S. government. Review expenses are paid primarily through application fees (see Exhibit 5-3); partial support for the reviews is provided by the Foundation for the Malcolm Baldrige National Quality Award.

After the review, applicants receive feedback reports prepared by members of the board of examiners. These reports critique the application against the model. Generally, companies with scores around 700 (out of a possible 1,000) receive site visits and thus gain more substantial insight. In 1992, the distribution of scores was 401–600 (34 percent); 601–750 (14 percent). There were none higher. Some companies arrange one or more consultations with outside experts before their application review. Some former Baldrige Award examiners perform this service. For our purposes, a management faculty member at a local college or university would be capable of handling the assignment.

National Purposes and Goals

Besides being the basis for making awards and providing feedback to applicants, the Baldrige Award criteria have three other important *national* purposes:

1. To help elevate quality standards and expectations across the United States
2. To facilitate communication and sharing among and within or-

Exhibit 5-3. Baldrige Award schedule and fees.

Schedule

Eligibility determination:	Mid-March
Application deadline:	Early April
Written reviews:	Mid-April through August
Site visit reviews:	September
Award announcement and ceremony:	October or November
Distribution of feedback reports:	November and December

Fees

Eligibility determination fee:	$50, nonrefundable, for all potential applicants
Application fee:	Under $5,000 for medium and large companies ($4,000 in 1993), and under $1,500 for small businesses ($1,200 in 1993). The fees are adjusted annually and cover all handling costs associated with distribution of applications and compensation of examiners for application review and development of feedback reports.
Site visit review fees:	Variable, depending on the number of sites to be visited, the number of examiners assigned, and the duration of the visit. Small-business applicants are charged half the rate for large companies in that year. These fees cover application handling costs, travel costs, and compensation of examiners for site visits and development of site visit reports.

---

ganizations based on common understanding of key quality requirements
3. To serve as a working tool for planning, training, assessment, and other uses (which is the purpose stressed here)

The Award criteria are directed toward two broad results-oriented goals: (1) to deliver ever-improving value to customers while maximizing overall productivity and (2) to increase the effectiveness of the delivering organization. The Award criteria are built on the following core values and concepts, which integrate overall customer and company performance requirements.

Core Values and Concepts

- Customer-driven quality
- Leadership
- Continuous improvement
- Full participation
- Fast response
- Design quality and prevention
- Long-range outlook
- Management by fact
- Partnership development (particularly with suppliers)
- Public responsibility

The Role of Financial Performance

The Baldrige Award has suffered a certain amount of embarrassment as a result of the financial difficulties encountered by some of its winners. This is what led to the major 1992 improvements in the Award criteria mentioned earlier, which focus on operational results and financial performance. For our purposes, this shift broadens the Award, making it a more comprehensive management model. There are still gaps, which will be identified later, but there is far less room for ineffective performance. The Award criteria now provide:

- Emphasis on quality factors and management actions that lead to better market performance, market share gain, and customer retention
- Emphasis on improved productivity, asset utilization, and lower overall operating costs
- Support for business strategy development and business decisions

The focus on superior offerings and lower operating costs establishes a route to improved financial performance through the delivery of superior overall value. Delivering superior value also supports other business strategies such as pricing: It creates the possibility of offering price premiums or competing by means of lower prices. Either strategy may enhance market share and asset utilization and may also contribute to improved financial performance.

Examples of applications of the Award criteria to business decisions and strategies include:

- Quality management of the information used in business decisions and strategy to include scope, validity, and analysis
- Quality requirements of niches, new businesses, target export markets
- Quality status of acquisitions, with key benchmarks
- Analysis of societal, regulatory, economic, competitive, and risk factors that may bear upon the success or failure of a strategy
- Development of scenarios built around possible outcomes, which include risk of failure, probable consequences of failure, and management of failure
- Lessons learned from previous strategy developments within the company or available through research

The Award criteria and the evaluation system take into account market share, customer retention, customer satisfaction, productivity, asset utilization, and other factors that contribute to financial performance.

The criteria do *not* call for financial information such as quarterly or annual profits for several reasons:

- Short-term profits may be affected by such factors as accounting practices, business decisions, write-offs, dividends, and investments.
- Some industries historically have higher profit levels than others.
- The time interval between quality improvement and overall financial improvement depends on many factors; it varies from industry to industry and even among companies in the same industry.
- Financial performance depends in part on the quality performance of competitors, which the Award process cannot measure directly. The inclusion of aggregate financial indicators would place applicants in the most competitive businesses at a disadvantage.
- Financial performance depends on many external factors; such conditions and cycles do not have the same impact on all companies.

For the first time, the 1992 Guidelines presented a model linking the seven examination categories together (see Exhibit 5-4). The categories model has four basic elements:

Exhibit 5-4. Baldrige Award criteria framework (dynamic relationships).

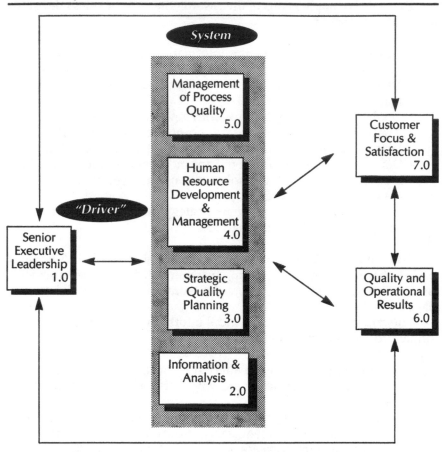

- Customer Satisfaction
- Customer Satisfaction
  Relative to Competitors
- Customer Retention
- Market Share Gain

- Product & Service Quality
- Productivity Improvement
- Waste Reduction/
  Elimination
- Supplier Quality

The Baldrige Award Examination Categories Model

1. *Driver.* Senior executive leadership creates the values, goals, and systems and guides the sustained pursuit of quality and performance objectives.
2. *System.* Comprises the set of well-defined and well-designed processes for meeting the company's quality and performance requirements.
3. *Measures of progress.* Provide a results-oriented basis for channeling actions toward delivering ever-improving customer value and company performance.
4. *Goal.* The basic aim of the quality process is the delivery of ever-improving value to customers.

The following method of displaying the categories and items according to scoring weight has proved to be a quick and effective way to see where the gold is buried. The fifteen items marked with an asterisk have scores of 35 and above and account for 75 percent of the 1,000 points.

Categories According to Scoring Weight

7.0	*Customer Focus and Satisfaction (300 total)*
7.4	Customer Satisfaction Results (85) *
7.5	Customer Satisfaction Comparison (70) *
7.1	Customer Relationship Management (65) *
7.3	Customer Satisfaction Determination (30) *
7.6	Customer Expectations, Current and Future (35) *
7.2	Commitment to Customers (15)

6.0	*Quality and Operational Results (180 total)*
6.1	Product and Service Quality Results (70) *
6.2	Company Operational Results (50) *
6.4	Supplier Quality Results (35) *
6.3	Business Process and Support Service Results (25)

4.0	*Human Resources Development and Management (150 total)*
4.2	Employee Involvement (40) *
4.3	Employee Education and Training (40) *
4.4	Employee Performance and Recognition (25)
4.5	Employee Well-Being and Satisfaction (25)
4.1	Human Resources Planning and Management (20)

5.0	*Management of Process Quality (140 total)*
5.1	Design and Introduction of Quality Products and Services (40) *

5.2   Process Management: Product and Service Production and Delivery Processes (35) *

5.3   Process Management: Business Processes and Support Services (30)

5.4   Supplier Quality (20)

5.5   Quality Assessment (15)

1.0   Leadership (95 total)

1.1   Senior Executive Leadership (45) *

1.2   Management for Quality (25)

1.3   Public Responsibility and Corporate Citizenship (25)

2.0   Information and Analysis (75 total)

2.3   Analysis and Uses of Company-Level Data (40) *

2.2   Competitive Comparisons and Benchmarking (20)

2.1   Scope and Management of Quality and Performance Data and Information (15)

3.0   Strategic Quality Planning (60 total)

3.1   Strategic Quality and Company Performance Planning Process (35) *

3.2   Quality and Performance Plans (25)

Using the Baldrige Model

Consider the seven key categories of the Baldrige Award in the same order as above. Determine which are the greatest present strength(s) in your organization, most useful in terms of improving your organization, and most challenging for your organization to accomplish.

Read through the section of the current Award Guidelines that contains the categories, examination items, and areas to address. Select those areas that are not covered in ISO 9000 or the Deming Prize Checklist; most fall under leadership, human resources development and management (note that training has had extensive coverage), and customer focus and satisfaction. The main criterion for selection continues to be congruence with company mission and objectives.

Next, go through the dimensions of ISO 9000 and the Deming Prize Checklist that *overlap* the Baldrige Award in some way; they may present opportunities to strengthen your system. Analyze and tighten the specific content and make the appropriate entries on your Master Manual tracking sheets, by organization.

Because of the complexity and detail of the Baldrige Award, this procedure will be conducted again later. One pass through it will probably not glean all that it has to offer.

Exhibit 5-5 presents a set of analytical tools to be used at the level of the examination items and areas to address in Categories 1 (Leadership) and 4 (Human Resource Development and Management). Although tremendously important, these categories may be unfamiliar to some; therefore, it is useful to set them apart for special attention. Over the years, there have been numerous failures to get and keep top-notch programs going. Often the root cause has been lack of support by the leadership and low levels of involvement on the part of people. The Baldrige Award has dealt with these two considerations.

Exhibit 5-5 provides an example of a methodology that might be useful for accomplishing a detailed analysis of the various dimensions in the Baldrige model and simultaneously conducting an evaluation of the status of these areas in your organization. These worksheets can be used within your organization to obtain needed input on a "wall-to-wall" basis. Their use will support an Award application initiative by providing the structure and basis for analysis and reporting.

Although you have already reviewed the examination items and areas to address, go through the Leadership and the Human Resource Development and Management sections again, adding your evaluation of the *status* of the areas from the worksheets. Adjust the tracking pages in your Master Manual. As appropriate, circulate the worksheets for reactions and comments by others. Consider creating local worksheets for other examination categories to enhance the quality of your Master Manual. Accumulate your notes on the transition/transformation and communication prompts by examination category for use in later launch phase activities when your system is installed.

Summary

The Baldrige Award model is a management breakthrough; it has been accepted as a sound way to conduct the business of a company. The model is still somewhat incomplete and has its share of critics, but years of writing and research by management experts have yielded nothing as important as the Baldrige Award in terms of codifying the management process. Although the Baldrige Award was advanced as a solution to quality assurance challenges, it has always been broader, with its total quality, continuous improvement, and customer-oriented philosophy.

(Text continues on page 99)

Exhibit 5-5. Analysis of Categories 1 and 4.

This worksheet is to be used to assess the status of the areas to be addressed in Category 1 (Leadership) and Category 4 (Human Resource Development and Management) in your organization. "Needs work" signals that the area is not up to standard for day-to-day operations. "Basically Sound" means that the area meets a typical day-to-day standard but has not yet been given the special effort needed to build a quality management system; it doesn't specifically support a quality effort. "Supports Quality Standard" means that the areas are set up to sustain or enhance quality initiatives; the term *quality* is found frequently in policies and procedures related to it. "World-Class" means that the area will beat the best—that there is a high likelihood that breakthrough thinking has been applied and that the area reflects sound, systematic, consistent, and integrated methods; full deployment; and excellent results.

The worksheet entries for "Transition/Transformation" and "Communication" decisions are prompts to which the person doing the analysis should respond. They are fundamental considerations and are best dealt with at the time of the analysis of the area of interest.

The relation to the Master Manual mechanism is straightforward: Each area identified by a letter and each of its separate elements (usually no more than two or three) are candidates for a tracking page in the Master Manual.

1.0   Leadership   (95 points)

1.1   Senior Executive Leadership   (45)

	Needs Work	Basically Sound	Supports Quality Standard	World-Class
a. Senior executives' leadership, personal involvement, and visibility are clear in quality-related activities:				
—Reinforcing a customer focus	___	___	___	___
—Creating quality values	___	___	___	___
—Setting quality expectations	___	___	___	___
—Planning and reviewing quality progress	___	___	___	___

	Needs Work	Basically Sound	Supports Quality Standard	World-Class
—Communicating with employees	____	____	____	____
—Recognizing employee contributions	____	____	____	____
—Meeting with customers, suppliers	____	____	____	____
—Becoming knowledgeable about competitor quality (domestic, international)	____	____	____	____
b. Senior executives build customer-focused quality values into the organization's leadership processes and communicate quality consistency inside and outside the company.	____	____	____	____
c. Senior executives provide leadership and communicate the need for quality excellence to managers and supervisors.	____	____	____	____
d. Senior executives evaluate and improve the effectiveness of their personal leadership and involvement.	____	____	____	____

Transition/transformation decisions, action plan (start, stop, modify):

(continues)

Exhibit 5-5. Continued.

Communication decisions:

1.2   Management for Quality   (25)

	Needs Work	Basically Sound	Supports Quality Standard	World-Class
a. Customer focus and quality values are translated into requirements for all levels of management and supervision.	____	____	____	____
Quality roles and responsibilities are known within own units, in cooperation with others.	____	____	____	____
b. Organizational structures are analyzed to most effectively and efficiently serve customer quality, innovation, and cycle time objectives (show indicators, benchmarks, and other bases used for evaluating and improving structures).	____	____	____	____
c. Reviews are scheduled and conducted focusing on both organizational and unit quality plans and performance (show types, frequency, and content).	____	____	____	____

	Needs Work	Basically Sound	Supports Quality Standard	World-Class
Actions taken to assist units not performing according to plans or goals are described.	___	___	___	___
d. There are key methods and indicators to evaluate and improve awareness and integration of quality values at all levels of management and supervision.	___	___	___	___

Transition/transformation decisions, action plan (start, stop, modify):

Communication decisions:

1.3   Public Responsibility   (25)

	Needs Work	Basically Sound	Supports Quality Standard	World-Class
a. Quality policies and practices include public responsibilities such as:				
—Business ethics	___	___	___	___
—Public health and safety	___	___	___	___

(continues)

Exhibit 5-5.   Continued.

	Needs Work	Basically Sound	Supports Quality Standard	World-Class
—Environmental protection	___	___	___	___
—Waste management	___	___	___	___
The following are summarized: (1) how risks are identified, analyzed, and minimized; (2) quality goals and how set; (3) improvement methods; (4) quality indicators by area; (5) how and how often progress is reviewed.	___	___	___	___
b. Quality awareness and sharing are promoted with external groups.	___	___	___	___
c. Company looks ahead to anticipate public concerns and assess their impact.	___	___	___	___
d. Company leads as a corporate citizen.	___	___	___	___
e. Company responds to any sanctions received.	___	___	___	___

Transition/transformation decisions, action plan (start, stop, modify):

Communication decisions:

4.0   Human Resource Development and Management
       (150 points)

4.1   Human Resource Planning and Management   (20)

	Needs Work	Basically Sound	Supports Quality Standard	World-Class
a. Plans derive from quality and performance plans:				
—Short term (1–2 years):				
Education, training, skill development	—	—	—	—
Recruitment	—	—	—	—
Flexibility in work organization	—	—	—	—
Involvement	—	—	—	—
Empowerment	—	—	—	—
Compensation	—	—	—	—
Recognition	—	—	—	—
—Long term (+3 years):				
Education, training, skill development	—	—	—	—
Recruitment	—	—	—	—
Job reengineering	—	—	—	—
Involvement	—	—	—	—
Empowerment	—	—	—	—
Compensation	—	—	—	—
Recognition	—	—	—	—
b. Key quality, cycle time, other performance goals and improvement methods exist for:				
—Recruitment	—	—	—	—
—Hiring	—	—	—	—
—Personnel actions	—	—	—	—
—Personnel services	—	—	—	—

(Specify indicators used in improvement.)

(continues)

Exhibit 5-5.   Continued.

	Needs Work	Basically Sound	Supports Quality Standard	World-Class
c. Organization evaluates and uses all employee-related data to improve the development and effectiveness of the entire work force.	____	____	____	____

(Describe how processes address all types of employees—e.g., exempt-nonexempt, union represented; various demographics.)

[*Note:* Consider mechanisms for promoting cooperation, such as]:

	Needs Work	Basically Sound	Supports Quality Standard	World-Class
• Internal customer/ supplier techniques or other internal partnerships	____	____	____	____
• Labor-management initiatives, such as a partnership	____	____	____	____
• Recognition system creation or modification	____	____	____	____
• Mechanisms for increasing or broadening employee responsibilities	____	____	____	____
• Developing employee skills beyond current assignment through job redesign	____	____	____	____
• Creation of high-performance teams	____	____	____	____
• Education and training initiatives	____	____	____	____

Transition/transformation decisions, action plan (start, stop, modify):

Communication decisions:

4.2   Employee Involvement   (40)

	Needs Work	Basically Sound	Supports Quality Standard	World-Class
a. Organization uses management practices and specific mechanisms (e.g., quality teams, suggestion systems) to promote employee contributions to quality, individually and in groups.	——	——	——	——
Organization systematically provides feedback on inputs (Baldrige Award report summarizes how and when).	——	——	——	——
b. Organization takes action to increase employee authority to act (empowerment), employee responsibility, and innovation, which is based on organizational needs for all employee categories (e.g., exempt-nonexempt, union represented). Baldrige Award report summarizes principal goals for all categories.)	——	——	——	——

(continues)

Exhibit 5-5. Continued.

	Needs Work	Basically Sound	Supports Quality Standard	World-Class
c. Organization uses key indicators to evaluate the extent and effectiveness of involvement by all categories and types of employees (Baldrige Award report shows how the key indicators are used).	___	___	___	___
d. Organization tracks trends and current levels of involvement by all categories (and types) of employees, using the most important (key) indicator(s).	___	___	___	___
Transition/transformation decisions, action plan (start, stop, modify) Communication decisions:	___	___	___	___

Transition/transformation decisions, action plan (start, stop, modify):

Communication decisions:

4.3   Employee Education and Training   (40)

	Needs Work	Basically Sound	Supports Quality Standard	World-Class

a. Organization assesses
   the need for type and
   amount of quality edu-
   cation and training by
   all categories of employees (report describes relevance to plans; needs
   of employees; work un-
   its with access to skills
   in problem analysis and
   solving, process simplification):

	Needs Work	Basically Sound	Supports Quality Standard	World-Class
—Basic quality aware- ness	___	___	___	___
—Leadership	___	___	___	___
—Problem solving	___	___	___	___
—Meeting customer re- quirements	___	___	___	___
—Process analysis	___	___	___	___
—Process simplification	___	___	___	___
—Waste reduction	___	___	___	___
—Cycle time reduction	___	___	___	___
—Effectiveness/effi- ciency	___	___	___	___
Effective methods are used to deliver educa- tion and training.	___	___	___	___
Organization ensures on-the-job reinforce- ment of use of knowl- edge and skills.	___	___	___	___

b. Organization maintains
   summary and trend data
   of quality education and
   training:

(continues)

Exhibit 5-5. Continued.

	Needs Work	Basically Sound	Supports Quality Standard	World-Class
—Quality orientation of new employees	——	——	——	——
—Percent of employees receiving quality and related education and training annually, by employee category	——	——	——	——
—Average hours of quality education and training annually, per employee	——	——	——	——
—Percent of current employees who have received quality education and training	——	——	——	——
—Percent of employees who have received education and training in design quality and statistical and other quantitative problem-solving methods	——	——	——	——
c. Organization has key methods and indicators to evaluate and improve the effectiveness of its quality and related education and training for all categories and types of employees. (Describe delivery effectiveness, on-job performance improvements, and employee growth.)	——	——	——	——

Transition/transformation decisions, action plan (start, stop, modify):

Communication decisions:

4.4   Employee Performance and Recognition   (25)

	Needs Work	Basically Sound	Supports Quality Standard	World-Class
a. Performance, recognition, promotion, compensation, reward, and feedback processes for individuals and groups (including managers) support the organization's quality and performance objectives.	——	——	——	——
Quality is specifically reinforced relative to short-term financial considerations.	——	——	——	——
Employees contribute to the organization's performance and recognition approaches.	——	——	——	——
b. Organization tracks trends in reward and recognition by employee category for contributions to quality and performance objectives.	——	——	——	——

(continues)

Exhibit 5-5.   Continued.

	Needs Work	Basically Sound	Supports Quality Standard	World-Class
c. Organization has key methods and key indicators to evaluate and improve its performance and recognition processes. (Describe cooperation involved, participation by all employee categories and types, and employee satisfaction.)	____	____	____	____

Transition/transformation decisions, action plan (start, stop, modify):

Communication decisions:

4.5   Employee Well-Being and Morale   (25)

	Needs Work	Basically Sound	Supports Quality Standard	World-Class
a. Quality improvement activities integrate well-being and morale factors (e.g., health, stress, safety, ergonomics, satisfaction). (Report summarizes key improvement goals and methods for each relevant and important factor.)	____	____	____	____

	Needs Work	Basically Sound	Supports Quality Standard	World-Class
Causes of accidents and work-related health problems are determined, and adverse conditions prevented.	____	____	____	____
b. Organization maintains mobility, flexibility, and retraining to:				
—Support employee development	____	____	____	____
—Accommodate changes in technology, improved productivity, changes in work processes, or company restructuring	____	____	____	____
c. Organization makes special services, facilities, and opportunities available (e.g., counseling assistance; recreational, cultural activities, non-work-related education; outplacement).	____	____	____	____
d. How and how often levels of employee satisfaction are determined.	____	____	____	____
e. Trends in key indicators of well-being and morale are also tracked and analzyed for quality implications:				
—Satisfaction	____	____	____	____
—Safety	____	____	____	____
—Absenteeism	____	____	____	____
—Turnover	____	____	____	____

(continues)

Exhibit 5-5.   Continued.

	Needs Work	Basically Sound	Supports Quality Standard	World-Class
—Attrition for customer- contact personnel	___	___	___	___
—Grievances	___	___	___	___
—Strikes	___	___	___	___
—Worker compensation	___	___	___	___
—Other: _____	___	___	___	___

(Report explains important adverse results, if any; describes how root causes were determined and corrected or current status.)

Organization compares results on most signifi- cant indicators with in- dustry averages, leaders, and other key bench- marks.	___	___	___	___

Transition/transformation decisions, action plan (start, stop, modify):

Communication decisions:

In spite of changes in language and scoring, earlier versions of the Baldrige model are recognizable in today's version. Organizations that adopted the practice of using surveys to track progress against Baldrige Award dimensions can continue to do so, particularly if they started with the 1991 Guidelines. It is now time to minimize annual changes to the Guidelines to allow benchmarking and tracking of the Baldrige Award process itself.

The Baldrige Award is a matter of saving the best for last in terms of adding depth and breadth to the Master Manual as the mechanism for building an overall quality management system.

Individual copies of the current Baldrige Award Application Guidelines are available free of charge from:

Malcolm Baldrige National Quality Award
National Institute of Standards and Technology
Route 270 and Quince Orchard Road
Administration Building, Room A537
Gaitherburg, MD 20899
Fax: 301–948–3716   301–975–2036

Multiple copies may be ordered in packs of ten from:
American Society for Quality Control
Customer Service Department
P.O. Box 3066
Milwaukee, WI 53201–2036
Fax: 414–272–1734   800–952–6587

One pack costs around $25 plus postage and handling. Major credit cards are accepted.

6

System Documentation: The Right Kind, the Right Amount

The vital issue when introducing a quality management system is not in coping with the traditional resistance to change—but in identifying and applying effective techniques for managing it.

Effective Techniques for Managing Change

One powerful technique is to create a Protocol. A Protocol is a working publication that generally communicates intentions, describes how activities will be approached, and helps serve as a reference when conflicts develop. The Master Manual, which is a key concept as the overall quality manual in ISO 9004 (see Chapter 3), can serve as the Protocol. It can be an effective and inexpensive communication vehicle. If it's in a loose-leaf format, it can be changed easily, and pages can be used selectively to create other manuals by vertical or horizontal organizational slice. Or you can orchestrate a buildup from a small number of pages in a pilot situation to a full-blown package addressing the organization's mission and objectives.

There are two other highly effective techniques that add significant elements to a successful change. The first is to create a personal log of individual and team ideas and self-measurements that travels with each employee or associate in the form of a pocket notebook or resides in a personal computer in the form of an electronic file. The second is to develop worksheets that facilitate comparisons between your situation and that in other organizations (benchmarking) and to track your progress against other highly regarded organizations, either internal or external.

Therefore, to create the documentation necessary to make your quality management system a reality, you need three locally developed publications:

1. *Master Manual*. It records and tracks organizational-level quality management elements of the TQM Trilogy.
2. *TQMetrics*. It records and tracks individual and team contributions to the Trilogy quality management elements. It is also a convenient place to note improvement ideas.
3. *Benchmarking worksheets*. These establish how good an organization is in selected areas relative to internal and/or external organizations that are perceived to be models of excellence, or "world class."

Managing the Introduction of Change

Introducing change requires a clear view of objectives so that you can go forward with confidence and communicate your intentions to others. In fact, identification of objectives is a prerequisite for the effective management of any activity. The three documents listed above are all you need to create your quality management process. The key is to pull the appropriate management dimensions out of the Trilogy, convert them into objectives, and incorporate them into the three publications. That way, you will capture the significant management knowledge available today. Here is your opportunity to create a QMS from perhaps the most respected and accepted resources ever assembled.

We will provide an outline of the three publications you'll need (see Chapter 9). Clearly, you must tailor each of them to fit your organization—if not immediately, then certainly after you've had some experience with them.

Dealing With Resistance

As important as it is to have a Protocol to help you organize, communicate, and manage conflict, there is a huge risk associated with having Master Manual documentation. The risk is simply having too much material that is also too complicated and too confining. We've all been in situations where policies and procedures totally frustrated flexibility and creativity. That may be appropriate for technical procedures, such as how to run a process operation at a refinery or an assembly line in a manufacturing plant, but that's not what a sound management system needs. In a number of organizations, the demand for process reliability has created a rigid, nonresponsive environment. But flexibility, creativity, and responsiveness are the essentials of successful quality management systems.

Classic examples of publication rigidity include army regulations, university catalogs, and "generally accepted" accounting procedures. This is not to say that there is *no* flexibility in these publications, but they certainly carry that stereotype. When you embark on the installation of your quality management system, you must plan for potential negative stereotyping of your documentation efforts. In any change effort, there are *always* those who would prefer that the change not take place, and for legitimate reasons from their perspective. There may be a fear of the unknown and a fear of failure in the new situation. New language and new symbols can add confusion. A diverse work force may be particularly vulnerable with respect to communication issues. This means that careful change management steps are needed to diminish the likelihood of resistance.

How do you plan to deal with resistance? First, review the Evergreen System (see Chapter 11). Next, consider the following twelve suggestions:

1. Ask a lot of questions and use formal assessments to determine where people disagree with respect to the documentation concept. Take the results into account: Accommodate. The one key conviction of successful managers of change is, "There is more than one way to skin a cat."
2. Relate the current management system change to other previous successful changes.
3. Promise a better world as a result of the approach—and deliver. Show off early successes.
4. Work on employee and associate needs and motives that the concept will support; don't neglect simple things such as pride, envy, and greed.
5. Introduce anxiety about what the organization's future will be without the change the documentation brings, if warranted.
6. Keep the documentation development and publishing specifics as simple as possible; if you can't communicate your plan on one sheet of paper or describe it in two minutes, you're in trouble.
7. Identify what is valuable and rewarding in accepting the docu-

mentation for the individuals involved. Make the connection clear.

8. Establish where organizationwide involvement is possible and practicable, and use it. Don't forget that manipulation is always transparent; if you can't respond to what you're likely to be told about your approach, don't play games.

9. Publicly demonstrate support by senior leaders; encourage trusted lower-level leaders to speak on the system's behalf. Pull in your markers.

10. Be willing to compromise; install documentation in phases so that there is always an opportunity to respond to criticism.

11. Eliminate the chance of frustration associated with having inadequate resources to accomplish what the documentation requires.

12. Introduce posters and slogans that highlight the need for continuous system improvement.

Keep this list handy; the twelve items work in almost any setting.

The Master Manual

Let's assume that you are starting with an empty three-ring binder that will become the master quality management manual for your organization. You may need several other smaller binders to allow publishing by segment or level. In any event, it is time to move forward in applying the Trilogy. You may believe that a special task force would be helpful or that it would make sense to delegate responsibility to one or more existing work teams. There is no reason for one person to do all the work, but there is every reason to have one person review and approve the final product.

The answers to the following questions will start you off in the right direction as you begin to create your Master Manual:

- Is the organization clear about its mission (or purpose) and key objectives?
- Has the organization developed an ambition to register under the ISO 9000 Series? If so, which Standard will be used?
- Will the organization ultimately want to compete for the Baldrige Award or an emerging equivalent?
- Realistically, is the reason for going forward at the moment a *quality* management system or a quality *management* system? What are the implications for a Master Manual?

- Has the organization decided on one or more pilot programs? If so, is the focus for each clear and circumscribed?
- Who should take the lead in pilot efforts? Are there "natural" leaders available?
- How can task forces and work teams contribute? Can a case be made for having a strategic task force develop a series of steps for Master Manual development and publishing?
- If there is a collective bargaining agreement in effect, what are the implications? How does the union feel about task force and team management approaches? Be sure to bargain actions relating to the agreement.
- What steps, in which sequence, must be taken to bring the Master Manual concept to reality?

The Master Manual as a Protocol

The ISO 9000 Series focuses primarily on traditional quality control and quality assurance issues, but ISO 9004 adds an important extra twist by recommending the provision of numerous guidelines across areas such as management, economics, marketing, and personnel. It suggests creation of the master Quality manual for appropriate management system documentation, but it does *not* recognize its value as an instrument for organizing and managing *change*. We know that the management Master Manual is a sensible and practical concept that works because it becomes the common frame of reference for the organization in terms of what, where, and by whom things will be done. It becomes the Protocol for introducing or refining the management system.

Do you need a special label for your Master Manual? Probably. In many organizations, it is difficult *not* to create one. But be warned: One of the first things that happens when there is a new initiative is label (or acronym) generation. We can't fight that; it goes on all the time. Our experience, however, is that label or acronym generation can be a two-edged sword. Having a special label makes it easier to introduce and communicate a new concept; it avoids splintered interpretations. But that same label also: (1) sets your new initiative apart as something different, when ultimately you want it to be just "the way we run the business," and (2) creates a rallying point for those who disagree with your motives or methods. In other words, acronyms can take on meanings far different from those their creators contemplated. Clearly, this decision requires some thought.

The Master Manual will almost always consist of several manuals. Each organizational element has its own Master Manual, from the lowest to highest. The concept is straightforward: Do a buildup by level. Each level has its own management system stored in a computer file or in a three-ring binder for easy editing. The degree of detail at the upper levels of the organization is a matter of choice. In one organization, everything that is generated at lower levels is in a binder, or series of binders, at the top level. In another organization, lower-level entries are consolidated into more general statements at or near the top level.

There should be a standardized form for recording items for inclusion (Exhibit 6-1) in order to avoid missing any essential data. Ultimately, the various forms at each level, or in each segment, are collected in the appropriate Master Manual. Experience shows that organizations almost always want to design their own forms.

At any level, the person responsible for the management system should be able to welcome visitors with a "tour" of the Master Manual to describe the contributions at that part of the organization.

The Master Manual and the TQM Trilogy

The Quality Manual recommended in ISO 9004 provides the documentation needed to support the achievement of a particular ISO Standard elected by an organization. But from the Trilogy standpoint, the Master Manual may be only the content *starting point* for the total management system; it is then expanded with consideration of the Deming Prize and Baldrige Award. This sequence makes sense if you plan to register under one of the ISO standards but still want to approach quality improvement through management system improvement. But if your primary goal is to create an improved management system or to compete at some point for the Baldrige Award, the MBNQA may be a logical starting point. In most cases, the Deming Prize Particulars are a logical ending point, given their relative narrowness in terms of a management system.*

To create the Master Manual, those responsible for the new management system comb through the Trilogy and select the dimensions that will advance the management process at their location. There is sufficient information in this book to make a good start, especially if a high level of detail can be saved for later. This makes good sense in the interest of simplicity of system introduction. Original materials can then be obtained from Trilogy sources when and as needed.

---

*The exception would be if the organization is anxious to register under ISO 9000; then the Deming Prize model could be considered second to strengthening the statistical issues involved.

Exhibit 6-1. Suggested format for Master Manual tracking sheet.

1. Organizational identification (e.g., unit, department).
2. Dimension number. Refer to the twelve organizational system dimensions listed in the chapter. If subcategories have been created, provide a place to enter these identifiers as well. The dimension number should be a part of the page numbering system (e.g., page 3-1).
3. The specific Trilogy element. Enter the specific location within the element (e.g., check ISO 9001; enter 4.5.1).

   _____ ISO 9001   _____ Deming Particulars
   _____ ISO 9002   _____ Baldrige Award
   _____ ISO 9003   _____ Other (e.g., state award)
   _____ ISO 9004   _____ Other (e.g., professional mandate)

   Location: _____

4. Description/label. That would be document control in ISO, supplier quality results in the Baldrige Award.

5. Specific item/activity language or paraphrase.

6. Responsible person.

7. Date of latest update.
8. Specific item/activity. This ties directly to TQMetrics and benchmarking:
   - *Purpose.* Appropriate documentation available when/where needed.
   - *Content.* Master Manual controls, process documentation controls.
   - *Status.**
   - *Organizations/groups involved.* Coordinate with publications.
   - *Target/expected performance; "gap" analysis.***
   - *Key date(s).* Review date, release date.

---

*We recommend using a coding system such as Needs Work, Basically Sound, Supports Quality Standard, and World-Class. This language ties into the scales used in the Baldrige Award leadership and human resources inventories in Chapter 5 and Exhibit 5-4.

**This section requires substantial local work and tailoring; it is where the "numbers" go if measurements are involved. Express in units used in the statistical controls involved, as appropriate.

Potential Scope and Staging

Consider how large and complex a comprehensive Master Manual can become. The number of pages could approximate the number of potential dimensions in the Trilogy, minus those that are locally irrelevant and those that overlap one another, plus those from other sources that are locally important. For example, a state-level award may add something to the overall model, as might the special considerations involved in criminal justice, health care, or higher education accreditation. Here is the Trilogy potential:

Source	Dimensions
ISO 9001	44 requirements
ISO 9004	51 guidelines (elements 0, 4, 5, 6, 18)
Deming Prize	63 particulars
Baldrige Award	89 areas

The number of items provides only a rough check. There is a wide range of detail related to each element listed. In many cases, three to five Master Manual worksheets are involved for any dimension; in a few cases, there are as many as ten. The criteria for selection of a Trilogy item for inclusion in the Master Manual are the organization's mission (or purpose), objectives, and priorities, which were established or reviewed during the strategic/operational planning process. For logical organization, the Manual should have twelve sections, one for each of the twelve organizational system dimensions recognized in the Introduction to Part Two:

1. Management leadership/operational performance/quality procedures/continuous program elements/wall-to-wall deployment
2. Market research/product-service planning/design procedures/ product-service development
3. Purchasing-procurement proficiency/contracting methods/supplier performance
4. Handling/labeling/storage/safety
5. Documentation/records/control procedures/policies/traceability
6. Human resources management/training/development/education
7. Transformation and added value (production-service process activities)
8. Process quality control/standards/quality results/benchmarking/ auditing

9. Inspection/testing/test equipment/tagging-logging/corrective action/control of nonconforming output
10. Packaging/handling/inventory procedures
11. Marketing/distribution/delivery/installation/operation
12. Customer service/customer satisfaction/guarantees-warranties

It makes sense to organize the Manual itself by creating a general title for each of the twelve overall dimensions, with subtitles (and tabs) for the specific topics within each dimension. This model can be tailored for particular organizations; it should be adapted minimally to reflect a product or service orientation.

The specific steps that individuals, work teams, or task forces take in developing a Quality Management Manual, and its appearance, will vary with mission and situation. It is important to make this a challenging and rewarding task, not a hassle. Everything here can run in phases, so unless there is another motive operating (such as the need to register under ISO 9000), moving gradually and flexibly—but firmly—makes sense.

There are two old sayings in the business of introducing change that tell quite a story: "nibble and gnaw" and "there's more than one way to skin a cat." They speak to the value of gradualness and flexibility. What about firmness? Experience tells us that senior leadership is critical in providing the discipline needed to create a QMS. *Senior* is a relative term; it's nice to have the CEO inspired, but others well down in an organization can create their own management system if they have some local authority and autonomy. Although it would be terrific if a new, more effective management system grew out of initiative and creativity at the lowest organizational level, that is not the norm. So far, the norm has been a push or encouragement from the top of the organization while processes are set in motion for involvement at the bottom.

The specific steps for assembling a Master Manual are as follows:

1. Divide your Manual into twelve sections with tabs with titles.
2. Pick a starting point, usually the Baldrige Award Guidelines for your quality management system.
3. Create a worksheet (or several) for each relevant Baldrige area of interest. Note that:
    • Pilot program(s) normally do not involve all areas of interest.
    • Design could give priority (in sequence) to areas of interest under Leadership (1.0), Human Resources Development and Management (4.0), and Strategic Quality Planning (3.0).
    • The process can be expanded when and as appropriate.

4. Create a worksheet (or several) for selected ISO 9004 Guidelines. Note that:
   - As above, pilot programs normally involve only a limited number of Guidelines.
   - Design could give priority (in sequence) to Element 4 (Management Responsibility), Element 18 (Personnel), and Element 5 (Quality System Principles).
   - The process can be expanded when and as appropriate.
5. Review the Deming Prize Particulars for those that will support local pilot management system objectives; prepare a worksheet (or several) for those selected, or edit those already in existence; expand the process when and as appropriate.
6. Assemble the preliminary version of the Master Manual.
7. Distribute copies to senior management and to the task force(s) and work team(s) involved.
8. Arrange for task force(s) and work team(s) to complete the worksheets specified in items 3, 4, and 5, and return them for review.
9. Continue to cycle the process until the appropriate number of Manuals is produced.
10. Distribute the Manuals for use; provide copies for the task forces and teams responsible for publishing TQManagement and TQMetrics.

The process of actually implementing the system (the who, how, and why) relies on the management Triad to which you were introduced in Chapter 1: TQManagement (the overall guide to the process), TQMetrics (the mechanism for recording ideas and measurements), and TQMeetings (the tools for conducting work group and task force interactions).

The following ten questions will help you assess the application of the Master Manual approach for your organization:

1. Who will be responsible for its design, introduction, and maintenance?
2. How many organizational elements by level will want or need a Manual?
3. How will the lower-level Manuals differ from those at the top of the organization?
4. When is the appropriate time to introduce the Manual concept?
5. Is there something similar in place now? Has there been something before? What is or was the reaction to it? What can be learned and applied?

6. How will any cultural changes be managed?
7. Is producing a preliminary "dummy" Manual a potential quality team or task force activity?
8. How can the Manual be used to improve productivity? Who will determine target levels of performance by item tracked?
9. How can the Manual be used to arbitrate differences of opinion on priorities and resource allocations?
10. How does the suggested format need to be altered to fit your situation and accommodate additional Trilogy (or other) input?

TQMetrics

TQMetrics, along with the other components of the TQ Triad, is described in Chapter 9. There you will find a complete content outline and a description of its intended use within the system. The Master Manual flows to TQMetrics, which is the vehicle for achieving the QMS objectives, and also to the benchmarking initiatives undertaken by the organization.

Benchmarking: Using Documentation for Comparison

Benchmarking is the systematic comparison of one organization's performance with that of a respected or world-class organization. That comparison is used to set improvement goals and drive improvement efforts. Benchmarking is an art that is making the transition into a science. Top-notch documentation is the foundation to effective benchmarking.

Objectives of Benchmarking

1. Accelerate the process of business change and understand the implications of change initiatives.
2. Develop strategic alternatives.
3. Develop realistic improvement objectives; the gap between internal and external practices creates a yardstick.
4. Achieve both breakthrough and continuous improvements in products, services, and processes.
5. Identify performance improvement enablers.
6. Develop customer satisfaction and a competitive advantage.
7. Adapt business process improvements and best practices of organizations recognized for excellence in execution.

Benchmarking is a process that can grow in scope and complexity. Initial efforts should *not* overwhelm the organization. To become comfortable with the process, use selected Master Manual items. For example, use the Baldrige Award employee education and training item from the Human Resources Development and Management category. This is an important management consideration and relatively easy to handle. Remember, benchmarking comparisons can be internal or external. If there is an internal opportunity, use it first to gain expertise in the process.

Here is a striking comparison, presented at the 1992 Society for Human Resource Management (SHRM) National Conference, of two companies that demonstrates how benchmarking can highlight improvement opportunities and motivate improved performance:

Area	Ford	Toyota
Purchasing agents	490	25
Material coordinators	492	7
Inventory (days)	14	2
Labor per car (hours)	40	16
Defects per 1,000 units	130	45

Though some benchmarking is done at the organizational and divisional levels, with the comparison being the measurement of products and services (Exhibit 6-2), the most effective comparisons are done at the level of the business process (Exhibit 6-3). At this level of detail, usually organized around work flows and flow diagrams, it is possible to find more comparison partners (since many support processes are essentially generic within and sometimes across industries), and the process "owner" and "members" can usually see immediately what can be done to improve and perhaps even exceed challenging or world-class examples that are uncovered.

The basic benchmarking approach for business processes cannot begin until an organization develops its own process descriptions, flowcharts, and metrics. At the process level, the financial accounting system rarely, if ever, has useful data on productivity, quality, and timeliness. The same is true of most staff groups.

Plan, Do, Check, Act

Here are the steps in benchmarking, organized in the familiar plan, do, check, and act model:

(Text continues on page 115)

Exhibit 6-2.   Product/service benchmarking.

Background Information _____ Date _____

_____

Company/division _____ Source _____

Contact _____ Title _____ Phone _____

Address _____

City _____ State _____ ZIP _____ Fax _____

Industry _____ Same ___ Related ___ Database ___

How/by whom qualified _____

Other lead(s) acquired _____

Phone interview/visit date(s) _____

Participants _____

Reciprocal commitment(s) _____

Function(s) involved/key word(s) for search _____

Master Manual (ISO 9004) reference _____

Objective/Target 1 _____

Objective/Target 2 _____

Objective/Target 3 _____

Repeat the following data section for each significant objective/target:

	Own Current Performance	*Benchmark Performance*
Units produced/service provided	_____	_____
Time factors (JIT?)	_____	_____
Cost(s) involved	_____	_____
	_____	_____

	Own Current Performance	Benchmark Performance
Machinery/other equipment	_____	_____
Layout considerations	_____	_____
Scrap/rework experience	_____	_____
Warranty/guarantee experience	_____	_____
Output delivered	_____	_____
Customer data	_____	_____
Other	_____	_____
Other	_____	_____

Valid comparison:
Yes ___ With conditions ___ No ___

	Own Current Performance	Benchmark Performance
Executive leadership actions	_____	_____
Employee involvement (overall)	_____	_____
Task force/team experience	_____	_____
Training investment(s)	_____	_____
	_____	_____
Health/safety considerations	_____	_____
Recognition provided	_____	_____
Reward(s) provided	_____	_____
Technology		

Stable ___ Influx ___ Note(s) _____

_____

(continues)

Exhibit 6-2. Continued.

	Own Current Performance	Benchmark Performance
Approach:		
Tools	_____	_____
System	_____	_____
Evaluation	_____	_____
Data/SQC	_____	_____
Prevention	_____	_____
Deployment:		
All	_____	_____
Partial	_____	_____
Results:		
Q/P levels	_____	_____
Q/P rate of improvement	_____	_____
Q/P breadth of improvement	_____	_____
Sustained improvement	_____	_____
Improvements derive from Q	_____	_____
World-class implications	_____	_____

Note: Q/P, quality and performance; Q, quality practices and actions.

Summary

Significant differences/gaps

1. _____   4. _____

2. _____   5. _____

3. _____   6. _____

Actions needed/deadline dates in response to comparisons (priority order)

1. _____ ___/___/___

2. _____ ___/___/___

3. _____ ___/___/___

Schedule appropriate task force/team meetings (identification/date)

1. _____ ___/___/___

2. _____ ___/___/___

3. _____ ___/___/___

Information hand-offs to other functions/locations _____

_____

Implications for Master Manual (by section/page) _____

_____

_____

Thank you sent ___/___/___ Data passed to clearinghouse ___/___/___

_____

Steps in Benchmarking

Plan
1. Select a process, product, or service (Master Manual).
2. Identify potential benchmark partners.
3. Gain partner cooperation in participation.
4. Select your representative and team members.
5. Analyze process (transformation) flow and measures.
6. Define inputs and outputs.
7. Document the activity.
8. Select dimensions to benchmark.
9. Determine data-collection requirements.
10. Develop a preliminary questionnaire.

Do
11. Collect internal data.
12. Perform any appropriate research.

(Text continues on page 118)

Exhibit 6-3.   Process benchmarking.

[Note that much of the demographic, internal data, and follow-up information on the form shown in Exhibit 6-3 can also be used to good effect here.]

Process name _____

Process description (50 words) _____

_____

_____

_____

_____

Title/name of responsible person(s) _____

_____

Other key participants (with time fraction) _____

_____

Process flow chart (attach diagram):

- Number of approvals _____
- Number of possible reverse loops _____
- Number of "handlings" _____

Specific starting point _____

Specific ending point _____

Key process deliverables _____

Process Metrics:	Used?	Specific Parameter(s)?	Number(s)?
Labor productivity	————	————	————
Capital productivity	————	————	————
Internal error rate	————	————	————
Customer reaction	————	————	————
Customer satisfaction	————	————	————
Cycle time	————	————	————
On-time delivery	————	————	————
Resource utilization	————	————	————
Unit cost	————	————	————
Innovation/creativity	————	————	————
Other	————	————	————
Other	————	————	————

Deployment

Done this way throughout the organization? ————————————

If not, where else done this way (if at all)? ————————————

————————————————————————————

————————————————————————————

Where done differently? ————————————————

————————————————————————————

In which way(s) differently? ————————————————

————————————————————————————

————————————————————————————

13. Plan data-collection activity.
14. Develop an interview guide/survey.
15. Collect preliminary data.
16. Conduct site visit(s); accumulate partner data.

Check

17. Aggregate data.
18. Normalize performance.
19. Compare current performance to partner data.
20. Identify gaps and root cause(s).
21. Write up best partner practices.
22. Identify performance-improvement enablers.
23. Assess adaptability of learning to own organization.
24. Project needed improvement(s); construct a time line, and catalog resources.

Act

25. Set goals to close, meet, or exceed the gap(s).
26. Assess Evergreen implications (see Chapters 2 and 11).
27. Modify improvement enablers to fit own culture, situation.
28. Gain support for improvements (see Chapter 7).
29. Develop action plan(s).
30. Commit resources.
31. Implement the improvements.
32. Monitor and assess progress.
33. Identify repeat or additional opportunities for benchmarking.
34. Recalibrate the benchmark.

There are potential pitfalls in almost any activity; benchmarking is no exception. Here are a few situations to avoid:

Potential Pitfalls

- Not benchmarking at all
- Not factoring internal constituent and partner expectations into studies
- Not involving process and/or product or service "owners"
- Having team members who are not committed to substantial effort
- Not following a systematic and reproducible procedure (sloppy preparation)
- Not making sure potential partners are fully qualified early in the activity
- Choosing to investigate areas that are not valuable or of limited value or not of interest to management

- Having unrealistic expectations as to time and other resources needed and length of time to reach final results
- Not being prepared to deal with "we're different" and "no resources" arguments
- Failing to recognize the need to continue to benchmark and recalibrate

Some Things to Think About as You Embark on the Benchmarking Process

- What value will be derived from the benchmarking process?
- Will only selected areas be benchmarked? Which one(s)? Which sequence?
- How will you get started? Does this have a special task force potential?
- Who might be tapped to be a benchmarking representative to other companies?
- What are the opportunities for internal benchmarking? Are there other divisions that have high-quality areas? What about affiliates within your corporation?
- Where will benchmarking funds come from? How much might be involved?

Benchmarking Support

The American Productivity and Quality Center (APQC) in Houston has created a benchmarking clearinghouse.

Benchmarking Clearinghouse Objectives

1. Promote, facilitate, and improve benchmarking as a science.
2. Improve productivity and quality in organizations all over the world.
3. Provide a central source of information useful to the benchmarking process.
4. Provide standard formats, templates, and protocols for entry and access.
5. Link analogous processes across industries.
6. Establish a network of contacts among members.
7. Create "best practices" and literature databases; optimize use of electronics.
8. Publish "how to" materials.
9. Make benchmarking easier, faster, and cheaper.
10. Conduct studies across industries, business sectors, and international boundaries.

11. Screen and qualify benchmarking partners.
12. Conduct training workshops and seminars and convene conferences and interest groups.

This is a welcome contribution. Redundant and nonproductive efforts are costly and time-consuming, and networking and partnering are difficult to establish and hard to maintain. APQC focuses on *generic* process benchmarking, which is frequently overlooked, as compared to *industry-based* benchmarking. It pays more attention to the gathering of process descriptions than to the gathering of measures, which are overemphasized and often break down when comparability is examined.

Part Three

Implementing a Premium Quality Management System

Having a vision or a dream is fundamental to successful implementation of organizational change. But then there's the whole issue of getting alignment on the part of people in the organization, obtaining buy-in, running a pilot, launching a process, and institutionalizing its operation. As important as the vision is, it will go nowhere without some serious, persistent, and informed steps to manage the change involved. Part Three focuses on three important tools that will help you implement organizational change: the experiences of others, teamwork, and the TQ Triad.

Industry Experience

You can learn a lot from industry experience with total quality management and quality management systems. This part provides a clear picture of important industry experience with change in a general sense and change as specifically related to quality management. The industry experience is organized into four parts:

1. Evidence of useful results
2. Caveats
3. Collective bargaining implications
4. Continuous process considerations

Teamwork

Teamwork and team processes are the keys to managing organizational change. The team structure provided here will get your quality management process in place and working with broad acceptance. It will energize creativity and generate needed quality improvements without being controversial. The goal is not self-managing teams but rather team management—a concept that covers a range of self-managing possibilities. It is fully congruent with quality management, but each concept can exist independently.

Change happens most successfully when the leaders involved have a clear idea of how to make it happen. The concepts needed for communicating to those around them need to be simple so that the buy-in process will cascade down through the organization. These concepts must be familiar and describable in practical, operationally oriented language. Having such concepts at hand makes a real difference in spreading new approaches that work. This enables the team process to flourish in the implementation and maintenance of change.

Also essential to task force and team progress is agreement in advance of any activity as to how progress will be measured. Once the vision is described and converted to missions or purposes, it is time to ask the question, How are we going to document our progress? This ties in directly with task force and team activities.

Consideration must be given, of course, to the appropriate chartering of your teams, given the pressure of collective bargaining agreements and the National Labor Relations Act (NLRA).

Most of all, managers working with teams on the installation of a quality management system need results, and they need ways to ensure results early on. Results energize most people, and they can certainly energize task forces and teams. Then change can move forward on the shoulders of success.

The TQ Triad

The TQ Triad is the practical, easy-to-communicate approach to change that facilitates widespread deployment and generates quick and replicable results. As you know, the Triad consists of:

1. *TQManagement*. The organization's tailored description of its intentions and preferred practices for its own quality management system
2. *TQMetrics*. The individual's logbook for noting ideas, tracking objectives and measures, and consolidating results from team meetings
3. *TQMeetings*. The team's guide and basic tool kit for effective interactions and the link to other teams both vertically and horizontally; how ideas are generated and creativity fostered; interlocking relationships that move outcomes of the task force through the organization

In the chapters that follow, you will find a host of ideas and suggestions on how to move forward confidently and successfully.

7

Incorporating Industry Experiences to Assure Management System Success

There is no shortage of information about TQM or about the Baldrige Award as a TQM vehicle. The initial shortage of information about the ISO 9000 Series at the start of the 1990s was overcome in the rush to register once the significance of registration became clear. There are articles in business and professional journals; there are many books other than this one; there are respectable professional journals dedicated solely to quality. The editorial focus of all of these has largely been on "traditional" TQM, which is basically a broad-scale quality assurance activity, but the up-to-speed publications are expanding their coverage beyond that position. For example, *Quality Digest* has a clear interest in management issues. But there is still not much organized information about total quality *management* systems.

One of the problems with a wave of enthusiasm for almost anything is sorting out what is substantive from what is hype. It is important to read the words carefully to see whether there are a base of experience and concrete recommendations involved.

This chapter consists of four sections:

1. Evidence of useful results
2. Caveats
3. Collective bargaining implications
4. Continuous process considerations

Evidence of Useful Results

The evidence of useful results of quality control and quality assurance programs is abundant; evidence of value is sketchy. There are two reasons for this: Fewer managers have seen the light regarding the management system approach. And research on an entire management system is complicated, expensive, and time-consuming. Following is a rundown on what constitutes rigorous organizational research so that you can be an effective critic of what you read, hear, and experience. Then you'll find some results of current studies and useful insights from CEOs and TQM conceptual leaders.

Substantive Research

The late Dr. Rensis Likert was the director of the Institute for Social Research at the University of Michigan for most of the 1960s and 1970s. For over twenty years, he devoted himself to analytical studies of management. In the mid-1960s he structured the Inter-Company Longitudinal Study (ICLS), a consortium of large, well-known companies, to determine once and for all how best to manage an organization. The approach involved exhaustive surveys of organizational practices and the tracking of financial performance and key personnel changes. Survey results were rigorously examined using a variety of statistical procedures. Progress in measurements was tracked, analyzed, and correlated with financial results and management changes. ICLS was designed to run for five years.

Each participating location surveyed 100 percent of its work force annually—25 percent each quarter. Survey feedback was followed by quality and productivity interventions wherever a need was indicated. Changes in measurements were monitored and correlated with changes in culture, practices, and policies. Over several years, productivity and quality results were very positive at all locations, although different in substance.

For example, the results were so good in one major automobile manufacturing company that it expanded the business-oriented organizational development process from two pilot plants to all plants in its assembly division. That's when it ran afoul of the union. The union argued that the bottom-line–related improvement activities were reshaping the relationship described in the collective bargaining agreement—in effect, cutting out or diminishing the union's role as representative of the workers. As recent articles in *The Wall Street Journal* demonstrate, that line of reasoning is a current issue in some unionized locations where TQM is being introduced. The auto company opted to tone down the content of the surveys. What started as a productivity and quality initiative became a "quality of worklife" process. It went from addressing bottom-line–related opportunities to dealing with parking lot and cafeteria issues. Not that these are unimportant, but they pale by comparison to the gutsy stuff that had gone before and that had a lot of frontline employees excited.

Likert formalized what was learned into a "systems" approach to management to replace what had been fragmented management processes. He described four types of management processes: System 1 represented an ineffective, exploitive, and authoritative level of management; System 4 represented a fully effective participative group and empowering approach to management. Likert's research showed that, on average, American managers were operating at around a 2.5 on a scale of 4. That's a great batting average, but it's not too hot for an industrial society that's being challenged by competition around the world.

In 1967, Likert's book *The Human Organization: Its Management and Value* was published. For its time, it had a highly unusual and insightful focus on the financial consequences of effective management of human resources. One section introduced the notion of "human resources accounting," which was designed to establish the financial investment associated with individuals and teams. This spawned a number of additional research activities but never caught on with the accounting profession. This may be the single most important reason why Likert is not the W. Edwards Deming of quality management. He is better known for the questionnaire scale (Likert scale) that he generated.

ICLS is an excellent "strawperson" for a description of sound research, but the research alternatives are almost endless: interviewing, focus groups, questionnaires, observation, records and reports, to name a few. The problem is that there has been precious little research on a management system level to match ICLS.

Current Research

PIMS Associates, a subsidiary of the Strategic Planning Institute, studies the impact of product quality on corporate performance. In 1986, PIMS reported that companies that provide premium-quality products and services have large market shares, higher return on investment, and an ability to charge premium prices. PIMS cautioned that the introduction of a quality improvement strategy reduces short-run profitability because of the costs involved and the disruption that accompanies change.

General Systems Company, which was founded by Dr. Armand Feigenbaum, the quality assurance pioneer, established that TQM systems consistently exceed industry norms for return on investment because of three factors:

1. TQM reduces the direct costs of poor quality—inspection, rework, warranties, and the like.
2. Improvements in quality tend to lead to increases in productivity.
3. The combination of improved quality and increased productivity leads to increases in market share.

In a *Business Week* special bonus issue,* Feigenbaum was quoted as having said, "Companies that embrace quality have an edge of up to ten cents on every sales dollar over rivals."

The American Society for Quality Control (ASQC) commissioned a study in 1989 that surveyed over 600 senior quality executives. The study reported that 54 percent of respondents were pleased with the results of their quality improvement efforts, with half of those reporting "significant results, including increased profitability and/or increased market share."

In 1992, ASQC reported the results of a study on compensation practices. A total of seventy-eight companies participated; some had been involved with TQM for years, and others were just considering involvement. Traditional "pay for performance" (individual incentives and merit programs, often with highly competitive ratings and rankings) continues to be the basic compensation philosophy and practice, in spite of challenges by some TQM advocates. Most compensation programs recognize and respond to achievement of financial results; quality contributions tend to be fed into nonmonetary recognition programs. There are several trends. One is to combine financial and quality considerations in compensation; another is a growing interest in creating team-based programs that would encourage high levels of team performance. This activity ties into a move toward "self-directed" work teams. The interim position is to change performance appraisal forms to include consideration of behavior that supports teamwork. The study urges consideration of Baldrige Award criteria in compensation, even if an organization is not competing for the Award.

Ernst & Young, with the American Quality Foundation (AQF), conducted a study reported in *The Wall Street Journal* (5/14/92) that looked at 4 industries, 4 countries, and a total of 584 companies. The companies involved used 945 different quality management tactics. U.S. companies fell notably behind German and Japanese companies in applications.

*"The Quality Imperative," 10/25/91.

The same story noted a recent McKinsey & Company study of thirty U.S. quality programs, two thirds of which had "stalled or fallen far short of yielding real improvement." The Ernst & Young study did not rank which tactics worked best, although the most successful programs typically included "strong personal involvement by senior executives, companywide awareness of strategic plans and goals, and an emphasis on simplifying process."

Reports in the trade books and journals, if they are rigorous, have a traditional quality assurance orientation. Certainly the "quality establishment" of AQF, ASQC, the Association for Quality and Participation (AQP), the American Productivity & Quality Center (APQC), and the Quality & Productivity Management Association (QPMA) has pressed for rigor in case studies, research initiatives, and journal articles. Unfortunately, many articles that managers read are at the "war story" level of sophistication. They are interesting but of questionable validity and generalizability.

The U.S. Government's 1991 Study

The Baldrige Award is a creature of the U.S. government. As noted, it promotes "awareness of quality . . . understanding of the requirements for quality excellence . . . and sharing of information." It has proved *not* to be a sure way to make or keep an organization profitable, at least with the criteria that were in place through 1991.

Management Practices: U.S. Companies Improve Performance Through Quality Efforts is a forty-two–page report that was produced in 1991 by the U.S. government's General Accounting Office (GAO) at the request of thirty congressmen led by the Honorable Donald Ritter of Pennsylvania (defeated for reelection in November 1992). His leadership created the self-supporting National Quality Council, a distinguished group of Americans who are helping the nation identify and act on critical quality issues. The Council charter is to play a key role in establishing "a *culture* of quality in American business, government, and industry."

The GAO Study examined twenty of the twenty-two Baldrige Award finalists through 1990 (before the 1991 tightening of the Guidelines and the 1992 incorporation of business performance considerations). The GAO also obtained input from eighteen other sources, primarily quality and productivity centers such as the APQC.

Results of Quality Initiatives

The GAO concluded that companies that "adopted quality management practices experienced an overall improvement in corporate performance." It took some time, however: On average, it took companies two-and-a-half years to improve their performance. Management allowed enough time for results to be achieved rather than emphasized short-term gains. The time span in smaller and service companies was less than the average; in larger companies it was more. The key results were as follows:

- *Enhanced financial performance.* Improved profitability, and increase in market share, total sales, sales per employee, and return on assets. Of forty observations, thirty-four had increases (85 percent) and six had declines.
- *Improved operating procedures.* Improved quality and lower costs, increased reliability and on-time delivery, and decreased errors, product lead time, and cost of quality. Of sixty-five observations, fifty-nine improved (91 percent), two declined, and four were unchanged.
- *Better employee relations.* Increased job satisfaction, improved attendance, decreased turnover. Of fifty-two observations, thirty-nine improved (75 percent), nine declined, and four were unchanged.
- *Greater customer satisfaction.* Improved ratings, increased overall quality perceptions and customer retention, and decreased complaints. Of thirty observations, twenty-one improved (70 percent), three declined, and six were unchanged.

Each organization developed its quality practices in a unique environment with its own opportunities and problems. There were no "cookbook" approaches, but there were common features in their quality management systems that closely followed the core values and concepts of the Baldrige Award (see Chapter 5). For the most part, they support the hypothesis that a quality *management* system should be the initial goal.

System Characteristics Fundamental to Success

The GAO Study identified the following characteristics as being associated with successful systems:

- *Managerial leadership.* Involvement of senior management and management of quality improvements to include integration into all-level planning.
- *Customer focus.* Use of customer-defined quality; restoring customer contact; applying new marketing concepts, such as "delighting" the customer; obtaining customer feedback, often with new techniques; recognizing internal customers.

- *Employee involvement and empowerment.* Implementation of supportive human resources practices; gaining employee commitment—usually tied in with a profound shift in management philosophy; providing training support—usually focused on awareness of quality issues and statistical procedures.
- *Open corporate culture.* Sharing of information, reduction of formal and informal barriers, encouragement of innovation, and achievement of high employee morale and job satisfaction.
- *Fact-based decision making.*
- *Partnership with suppliers.*

Recommendations for General Application

The Study found that some features of TQM are widely applicable to other organizations such as those concerned with health care, education, and service, and could result in improved performance. These features include the following:

- *Customer satisfaction.* This is critical, both externally and internally. Ultimately, customer satisfaction drives quality efforts.
- *Leadership.* Top executives must provide active leadership to establish quality as a fundamental value in the organization's management philosophy. They must establish a corporate culture that involves all employees in contributing to quality improvements.
- *Communication.* Quality concepts need to be thoroughly communicated and integrated across the organization.
- *Employee involvement.* Teamwork and training at all levels of the organization strengthen commitment to continuous improvement.

The last sentence of *Management Practices* is: "The results of the companies we studied indicate TQM systems are promising ways to strengthen a company's competitiveness in both domestic and world markets."

Warnings

The study also states: "While these data were sufficient to analyze performance trends, they were not sufficient to conduct a statistically rigorous analysis of the companies' performance under total quality management." You should also note, as indicated above in the key result areas, that there were a varying number of observations. All twenty companies did not participate in every category. You will also find in the detailed tables included in *Management Practices* that the percentage of improvements was in some cases so low as to be of little practical significance.

Nevertheless, despite its lack of rigor, the Study makes up for that with its commonsense conclusions and cautions about its validity and generalizations. It is a useful aid in understanding vital quality issues for managers who can't or won't read research reports.

You can obtain a free copy of *Management Practices* by calling the GAO at (202) 275-6241 or writing to:

U.S. General Accounting Office
P.O. Box 6015
Gaithersburg, MD 20877

CEO Observations

Managers typically attend a large number of meetings about quality, and they network extensively with people who are implementing quality programs. They hear their share of war stories, and after a while the stories take on a certain substance: That is, If you hear the same story often enough from credible people, it becomes believable. The success stories tend not to be shared as often. Collectively, here are the top ten actions that CEOs and other senior executives believe are needed to create an effective quality management system:

1. Demonstrate top-down commitment and involvement—*push*.
2. Set *tough* improvement goals, not just stretch goals.
3. Provide appropriate training, resources, and human resources backup.
4. Determine critical measurement factors; benchmark and track progress.
5. Spread success stories, especially about favorable benchmarking; always share financial progress reports.
6. Identify the costs of quality and routes to improvement; prove the case that quality costs decline with quality progress.
7. Rely on teamwork, involvement, and all-level leadership.
8. Respect the "gurus," but tailor every initiative for a good local fit.
9. Allow time to see progress, analyze the system's operation, reward contributions, and make needed adjustments.
10. Finally, recognize that the key internal task is a culture change and the key external task is a new set of relationships with customers and suppliers.

TQM's Conceptual Leaders

Three of TQM's conceptual leaders—W. Edwards Deming, Joseph M. Juran, and Phillip B. Crosby—took the lead in advocating new approaches to quality improvements and provided direction through their individual approaches to quality development or enhancement. The common thread is a respect, if not a driving desire, for the use of statistical approaches. Each has had a significant impact on the value attached to and the recent use made of statistical technology.

One caution must be offered when sifting through strongly held positions for inspiration or assistance: *Only those quality initiatives that have been custom-tailored for a particular organization and situation seem to work and to stay Evergreen over the long run.*

W. Edwards Deming

Deming's attacks on current human resources practices (e.g., performance appraisal, merit compensation) are well-known, but they are viewed by many practicing executives as too bound up in Eastern philosophy and tradition to be readily applicable in the United States.

He advocates a quality transformation through the application of the following fourteen points. Note that Deming makes important observations about supervision and management in points seven through twelve.

Deming's Fourteen Points

1. *Create a constancy of purpose for improvement of products and services.* This involves a long-run focus and dedication to innovation.
2. *Adopt a new philosophy: Poor quality is unacceptable.*
3. *Cease dependence on mass inspection.* Don't plan for defects; instead, improve processes and prevent defects.
4. *End the practice of awarding business on price tag alone.* Move toward trusted suppliers on a long-term basis. Change traditional purchasing practices.
5. *Constantly and forever improve the system of production and service.* Study the process; cut out waste. Improve quality and productivity, thereby decreasing costs.
6. *Institute modern methods of training on the job.* Use statistical methods to establish needs and verify successes. Focus on clearly defined concepts of acceptable work.
7. *Institute modern methods of supervising.* Remove managerial style and practice barriers that keep hourly workers from doing their

work with pride. Empower supervisors to inform management of corrections; action must follow.

8. *Drive out fear.* People must be able to ask questions, report problems, and express ideas.
9. *Break down barriers between departments.* The organization must work as a team. Multidisciplinary quality teams can provide valuable improvements.
10. *Eliminate numerical goals for the work force.* Eliminate targets, slogans, and exhortations asking for increased performance levels from workers. The organization, however, must have a direct goal focus.
11. *Eliminate work standards and numerical quotas.* Quotas adversely impact quality. Work standards practically guarantee poor quality and high costs; they are rarely exceeded.
12. *Remove barriers that hinder hourly workers.* People must know what good work is; supervisors must be responsive to frustrations about materials and equipment.
13. *Institute a vigorous program of education and training.* Training must be continuous because improvements alter staffing; all training must include basic statistical techniques.
14. *Create a structure in top management that will "push" every day on the above thirteen points.*

Here are the seven "diseases" that Deming sees as standing in the way of a quality transformation:

1. Lack of constancy of purpose
2. Emphasis on short-term profits (counter to constancy of purpose)
3. Personal review system (management by objective, performance evaluation, merit rating)
4. Mobility of management; job hopping
5. Use of only visible figures for management, with little or no consideration of figures that are unknown or unknowable (e.g., leadership, optimization of people, workers training workers)
6. Excessive medical costs
7. Excessive costs of warranty fueled by attorney fees

Joseph M. Juran

Juran offers a three-part system focusing on "fitness for use":

Juran's Three-Part System

1. Breakthrough projects
   - *Accomplish a breakthrough in attitudes.* Prove the need, focusing on cost of quality; establish the return on investment; create a climate for change.
   - *Identify the few vital projects.* Perform a Pareto analysis; establish priorities based on frequency.
   - *Organize for breakthrough in knowledge.* Incorporate a steering group for direction and authority and a diagnostic group for quality professional and line manager analysis.
   - *Conduct the analysis.* Have the diagnostic group develop hypotheses and experiment to find true causes, distinguishing those that are operator- and/or management-controllable; propose solutions to the problem.
   - *Determine how to overcome resistance to change.* Need must be established for key people; logic alone will not work; participation is essential.
   - *Institute the change.* Convince departments to cooperate with size of problem, alternatives, costs, expected benefits, anticipated impact on employees; consider time for reflection; provide for training.
   - *Institute controls.* Monitor solutions; correct sporadic problems.
2. Control sequence (comprehensive, from vendor relations to customer service)
   - *Optimize the cost of quality.*
   - *Establish needed professional staff entity.* Employ quality control engineers.
   - *Establish the feedback loop.* Establish an objective; define a unit of measure; set a numerical standard or goal; create a means of measuring sophisticated statistical applications; mobilize the organization to report.
   - *Repeat the action cycle.* Use actual as compared to standard; take action to close the gap.
3. Annual quality program
   - *Establish quality objectives.* Focus on items such as financial planning and the annual budget.
   - *Maintain the initiative.*

Phillip B. Crosby

Crosby describes quality as "conformance to requirements" and in the very long run, "free," with the goal of "zero defects." He believes that there are five phases in moving toward a quality system:

Crosby's Five Phases of a Quality System

1. *Uncertainty*. Quality is not recognized as a management tool.
2. *Awakening*. Quality is important, but action is put off.
3. *Enlightenment*. Quality problems are openly faced and addressed through a formal program.
4. *Wisdom*. Prevention is working well; early identification and correction are routine.
5. *Certainty*. Quality management is an essential part of organization; problems are infrequent.

Crosby also proposes a fourteen-point program for quality improvement. He expects such a program to be supported with management training and provision of operator training materials.

Crosby's Fourteen Points for Quality Improvement

1. *Management commitment*. This cascades from the top management down; there is a written policy.
2. *Quality improvement team*. Department heads oversee needed actions at company and department levels.
3. *Quality measurement*. Appropriate measures are established for every activity to identify needed improvements.
4. *Cost of quality evaluation*. It's important to identify where improvements are most profitable.
5. *Quality awareness*. Raise employee consciousness; message must be carried by trained supervisors and various media, such as films, videos, booklets, and posters.
6. *Corrective action*. Opportunities for this are suggested by above activities and employee discussions; problems should be resolved at supervisory levels or moved upward to management.
7. *Zero-defects planning*. This must be relevant for the company and its culture, and handled by ad hoc committee of quality improvement team.
8. *Supervisor training*. All management levels must be trained to implement their part of the quality program.
9. *Zero-defects day*. This signals employees that the company has a new performance standard.
10. *Goal setting*. Turn commitments into action; establish specific and measurable goals for individuals and groups; post goals and hold meetings to discuss them.
11. *Error cause removal*. Communicate upward on problems and frustrations; management should acknowledge within twenty-four hours.

12. *Recognition.* There must be public, nonfinancial appreciation for those who meet goals and perform in an outstanding manner.
13. *Quality councils.* This is where quality professionals and intra-departmental team chairpersons meet regularly to share.
14. *Doing it all over again.* Quality achievement is a never-ending process; renew commitments; bring new employees on board.

Caveats

Besides building a list of positive approaches to quality management systems (Exhibit 7-1), we need to build a list of caveats to take advantage of the experience around us.

Florida Power and Light

The experiences of the Deming Prizewinning Florida Power and Light (FPL) were discussed in Chapter 4, but the lessons to be learned are worth repeating here:

- You can lose sensitivity to employees and diminish good practices.
- Managers can become so intense about doing the right thing that they may ignore employee input or be unreceptive to suggestions.
- Quality system installation and maintenance may generate a formidable bureaucracy with an overemphasis on mechanics.
- You can spend a lot more on consulting fees and direct costs than is warranted.
- You could end up with counterproductive review and accountability processes.
- Training investments may favor quality mechanics over overall competency needs and the needs of those at or near the front line.
- You may be tempted by the inappropriate use of quotas and overworked metrics.
- If you rush into an initiative, you may neglect to build in an Evergreen strategy to ensure progress and avoid recidivism.

Many of these caveats have been published in business journals, but FPL senior executives have also been widely quoted at meetings and conferences.

Exhibit 7-1. Key dimensions of quality management systems.

Use this list to take inventory and clarify your situation. Manager and employee groups can use it to stimulate analysis and discussion. Rank the items (from 1 to 10) in each of the two columns to create a sharply focused picture of the challenges you might face. Make notes as to "why" as you go through the ranking process. Interpret the two columns as follows: *Need:* Conditions that need improvement to move your organization into a quality management system. *Difficulty:* Conditions that will be the most difficult to influence in moving toward a quality management system.

	Need	*Difficulty*
1. Providing all-level leadership, equipping people to perform	_____	_____
2. Knowing customer expectations	_____	_____
3. Providing customer satisfaction	_____	_____
4. Using strategic planning and following through	_____	_____
5. Developing and managing human resources	_____	_____
6. Involving and/or empowering employees/associates	_____	_____
7. Achieving world-class results	_____	_____
8. Establishing solid metrics and valid statistical procedures	_____	_____
9. Applying baselining and benchmarking techniques	_____	_____
10. Enhancing supplier relationships and contributions	_____	_____

Wallace Co.

Several caveats have been generated by the Baldrige Award-winning Wallace Co. experience. In 1990, Wallace became an instant success story and a model of the small organization in pursuit of the Baldrige Award. There were a couple of serous financial and operating problems, however. Wallace subsequently filed for reorganization, and recently it was sold.

Wallace won the Award under some of the early Guidelines, which were actually quite liberal. Back then, the application could contain an organization's fondest wishes and dreams; in other words, mere plans were sometimes perceived as "done deals." Starting in 1991, this was out of the question. Applicants had to specify exactly how, when, and where actions took place and results were observed.

Recent award-winning companies have tended to be relatively small (compared to, say, Cadillac Motor Car Company). Is it possible that being specific about quality initiatives and results on a wall-to-wall basis is just too much for a big company to handle?

Starting in 1992, the Baldrige Award considered a number of new business performance-related dimensions. Most people see this as an improvement, and most give Wallace credit for the change. What caveats come out of Wallace? Here are a few:

• *Be sure that training is on target and conducted on an economically realistic level.* Although we argue *for* giving priority to managerial and organizational issues, it is *not* useful to provide generic supervisor and team training if the objective is short-term company survival. Training costs money and takes people off the job.

• *Provide executive leadership in planning, communicating, coordinating, and making decisions.* The Wallace culture involved a lot of people who were "doing their own thing." There is a difference between empowerment and chaos. Also, Wallace's CEO commuted from another city, and while there was a quality committee, there was no clearly established deputy.

• *Maintain a human resources presence—not necessarily a high-flying professional, but someone with some expertise internally or externally.* Wallace had a human resources committee but no human resources manager, and there was little or no HR expertise on the committee.

• *Check your customer's wants and needs carefully.* Wallace generated a truly remarkable delivery guarantee without much consultation with customers. To meet its own perception of quality service and honor its guarantee, it spent a ton of money on premium freight charges. It turned out that customers did not universally need the level of commitment provided by Wallace. This kind of needless spending can be considered "industrial hara-kiri."

• *Control the company's operations.* It is fine to involve and delegate; it is risky to empower without appropriate controls. That management control function still has to be performed. Wallace authorized its people to make decisions that had financial ramifications and lost control of expenses. Find ways to have controlled empowerment. This is not an oxymoron; it can be done.

The Baldrige Fallout

Conferences, seminars, workshops, and institutes devoted fully or partially to quality and the Malcolm Baldrige National Quality Award abound and offer advice and counsel. Here are a few things to consider before applying for the Award, should you choose to do so:

• *The Baldrige Award is perceived as a rich man's game.* This comes from early reports of companies spending tons of money on staff to track and analyze metrics and on "training for all." An elaborate application effort is not a prerequisite for winning, however; one early winner (Globe Metallurgical) knocked off the application on a PC over a weekend. Curt Reiman, the Baldrige Award director, in commenting about the money spent by the 1991 winners, said that they "don't have that kind of money, but they do have tremendous energy."

• *The number of competitors seems to be running at around 100 companies each year.* Of course, the more competitors there are, the more challenging the preparation and application. Spending hundreds of thousands of dollars to crunch numbers and write applications just for the contest is clearly wrong-minded, but it may work: If, in fact, an organization actually benefits from the Award, the preparation cost quickly becomes a good financial and advertising investment. Time alone will establish Baldrige Award payoffs; since the Award has been in existence only since 1988, the broad-gauge management impact is inconclusive. The argument could be made, of course, that the reason is *micromanaging* quality assurance rather than creating quality management systems.

• *It has been said that Baldrige participation works only when there is a top-down emphasis and a lot of chief executive steam behind it.* Maybe so. It seems to have taken hold when organizations are in extreme business situations and the boss needs something to save the day, such as the Xerox model. But this doesn't have to be the case. Up to a point, any supervisor or team representative can pick up the current application Guidelines: He or she can set up small task forces to get up to speed on the details, inventory the organization's strengths, and identify gaps and then use a self-help approach to training; in almost any group of college graduates there will probably be someone with a statistical, and perhaps even a quality control, background. So far, so good. But then the need for upstream and downstream coordination becomes clear, and the stream goes over its banks. Resource needs that are not team-controlled—in the form of time, if not dollars—become obvious, and upper management has to become involved. Actually, TICICO (total involvement/continuous improvement/customer orientation) can work its way through an organization from both ends of a hierarchy very nicely; it does not have to be imposed from on high; and it is exactly what has to happen when there is a team management culture already in place.

• *Some key words related to the Baldrige Award are* all *(deployed throughout the organization),* how *(the 1991 Guidelines created an obligation to explain actions rather than intentions),* trend *(compiling* numbers *over time, which demands* tracking *and* benchmarking*), and* performance *(the 1992 Guidelines established a focus on organizational and financial results).* The effect of the improved models and criteria in the 1991-1992 Guidelines is clear: Large organizations have trouble making everything come together.

• *The belief is that no company that applies for the Baldrige Award loses, in that at minimum it will receive a professional critique of its application.* This is true *if* the organization scores high enough for a site visit; below that level, however, the "critique" simply feeds back the documentation submitted against the model. Don't expect more than you'll receive. You may want to do your own analysis (or use a third party to develop feedback against the model and prepare for the competition). For example, Federal Express hired a consulting firm to conduct three mock site visits. Such an analysis has a positive yield regardless of competition involvement or results; if need be, it can be done with internal resources.

• *There is only one guaranteed Baldrige "loser": the company that can't repeat the victory when it is eligible again after five years.* It will be interesting to see what winners do. Some may decide to rest on their laurels.

• *Scoring and judging are worrisome. Some examiners and judges trade in on their status and hire themselves out as consultants.* This is a major concern for NIST, which is trying to protect the Award's reputation. Cadillac's customer reputation (and its advertising subsequent to winning, which tried to spread the glory over all of General Motors) seemed troublesome. But the Award's credibility may not be damaged if the importance of quality trend data, as opposed to absolute levels of quality, is recognized. Along with other U.S. car manufacturers, Cadillac *can* show significant positive trends in quality. United Services Automobile Association (USAA), with its tremendous history of customer satisfaction, believes that its military atmosphere turned off its site visitors. Another possibility is that doing extremely well for many years simply does not produce a strong enough *positive* trend.

We can expect further shake-ups in the presentation of Baldrige

Award procedures and processes; we hope that the basic model and scoring will be frozen at some point long enough for substantive research.

Troubleshooting Your System

Take a look at the following "dirty dozen" warning signs of trouble and ask yourself whether they exist in your organization. If so, what is their impact? If not, how were they avoided?

Twelve Warning Signs of Trouble

1. Wandering quality teams and confused supervisors
2. Rampaging champions or loose cannons
3. Nonstatistical logic and decisions
4. "Not discovered here" or "we're different" syndromes
5. Too many classes—training that interferes with productivity
6. Punishment for those who "do the right thing"
7. Fear of demands to pad the "numbers"
8. Strained working relationships (among peers, teams, union)
9. Competition for ownership of ideas
10. Perceived inappropriate use of standards or criteria
11. Lack of, or misdirected, appreciation and recognition
12. The historian's argument that "this too shall pass!"

Collective Bargaining Implications

It is hard for a union leader to argue against improving quality, but implementing a quality management system can involve employee and management interaction relating to work practice issues. This means that the National Labor Relations Act (the Wagner Act) must be considered, and serious disagreements between management and labor are possible. For example, quality-team practices may be seen as a form of negotiation that does not include union involvement. The term *working conditions* in the Wagner Act describes an area in which collective bargaining is mandatory. *Conditions* has been defined in a number of ways; clearly, there is some risk that your union could construe efforts to improve quality practices as an area requiring collective bargaining. There can also be union questions about issues of team management and pay for union members who attend quality task force and team meetings outside the normal work schedule (an issue that has already been raised with the NLRB). It is clear that involving the union is essential in many situations; problems occur when management designs and implements the quality structures and practices unilaterally.

Many union leaders will endorse quality initiatives—even, depending on timing and other local considerations, providing for them in the collective bargaining agreement or in a "side agreement." Others may fight the initiatives because of a philosophical conviction or a shaky relationship with management.

If quality is related to productivity—as it should be—the union leadership may argue that a "speedup" is under way. What's a speedup? Do you remember Lucille Ball and Vivian Vance's classic candy factory episode in the *I Love Lucy* television series? The two women try to keep packaging candy as the conveyor belt in front of them "revs up" to five or ten times its normal speed. They start grabbing the candy wildly. Candy gets crushed; candy flies through the air. They get to the point where they're stuffing candy in their pockets and mouths to keep up with the line as it goes by. Unions have opposed any hint of a speedup for years, with good justification: It changes the meaning of the collective bargaining agreement. Clearly, it is better to figure out how to recognize and reward people than to try to get more for less.

As in any other dealing with a union, management often makes its own bed. If the union leadership has a good understanding of the economics involved in quality (which can add jobs), receives prompt and accurate information about changes, and is encouraged to become involved as a quality partner, the new ways of doing business should run smoothly. In complex situations, the collective bargaining agreement may need to be reopened for negotiation, but this is an unlikely requirement in most situations.

Considerations for Continuous Process Companies

People who write about quality being free make an interesting point: Doing something right the first time, all the time, doesn't cost a dime. So far, so good. But what happens when a quality improvement approach requires a capital investment, such as new or modified equipment? Then, in a continuous process environment, quality is not free; it also involves a new part of the company's operation—capital budgeting. Is the new approach affordable? The cost-effectiveness analysis will probably prove that it's essential, but company economics may say, "Check back in a couple of years." The effect on the people who came up with the idea will be disappointment and frustration. Perhaps you can convince your banker to let you buy what you can't afford by borrowing against anticipated savings.

Continuous Process Operational Characteristics

- The continuous process culture already values and uses numbers; the engineering and information sciences demand solid data.
- Critical path activities are monitored with varying degrees of precision; processes are measured and managed.
- People in continuous process operations may be isolated from suppliers and the process itself; computer controls make many key decisions.
- External customers may belong to a totally different type of operation and may be halfway around the world; internal customers can be very real.
- Continuous process organizations tend to train their select workers generously in time and dollars; apprenticeships are common.
- Operation teamwork focuses on coordination and cooperation; work does not move in pieces; it approximates project or batch activity.

Continuous Process Opportunities for Quality Management

- Total Management Quality is *total*; there is a real opportunity to pull an organization together and continuously enhance competitiveness.
- TMQ focuses on significant, order-of-magnitude improvements; the potential to enhance profitability is real.
- Continuous process organizations with a small work force, strong interdependence, smart people, and focused operations are perfect for introducing new systems.
- Continuous process organizations already embrace values of defect prevention and customer satisfaction; the transformations needed to energize creativity and become world-class are manageable.
- Many continuous process organizations have a history of organizational development or organizational improvement; this provides a solid starting point.
- Although earlier improvement initiatives may have focused narrowly on cost savings, TMQ makes it possible for a continuous process organization to work on multiple dimensions to transform its culture.
- Earlier initiatives may have "nibbled and gnawed," especially with unions around; TMQ can move forward broadly and aggressively.
- Empowerment and the countervailing risk-management concern are the major potential stumbling blocks to continuous process success; the risks may be unacceptable.

Continuous Process Distinguishing Features

- There may not be much empowerment with respect to continuous process streams—the equivalent of the production line in manufacturing—because of risk; other areas can go full speed in equipping and empowering people to act.
- If a significant change or improvement opportunity is discovered, it may take years and multiple trade-offs to find or apply the needed capital and make related system alterations.
- SPC (statistical process control), the major component of quality improvement in many installations, is probably already in place (often electronically) in potential continuous process improvement areas.
- Continuous process operations may measure and track streams differently from the way manufacturing units do; discrete units may not be the measure of choice.
- Nothing about continuous process operations limits total quality efforts, including the practice of fully deploying metrics throughout the rest of the organization.
- Nothing about continuous process operations limits the opportunities for installing continuous improvement processes.
- It is just as critical to prepare a continuous process organization and its people carefully to gain interest and avoid cynicism as it is in any other situation (even though much of what is to be added is seemingly already in place).
- Organizations must tailor supplier enhancement concepts to emphasize the importance of obtaining raw materials from other parts of the organization instead of from external suppliers (continuous process organizations are often horizontally and vertically integrated).

Summary

The key to success is to stay involved in the pursuit of valid information. Networking is a powerful tool; it involves sharing experiences with others who have similar interests. Then there are local and national professional association meetings; attendance at workshops and seminars presented by the American Management Association, American Productivity & Quality Center, and other responsible sources; along with programs and services offered by colleges and universities. The content can be useful; the networking can be magnificent.

Reading is a major tool for self-development. Your local bookstore has many texts covering related management quality approaches. Pick up some of the new or dedicated professional publications and journals: *Continuous Journey*, published by the American Productivity & Quality Center; *Quality Digest*, published by QCI International; *Quality Progress*, published by the ASQC. Traditional management resources include such respected general management publications as *The Harvard Business Review* (bimonthly) and *Business Week*. Specialized publications (using the human resources arena as an example) include *Training, Training & Development Journal, HRMagazine*, and *Personnel Administrator*. *The Wall Street Journal* (published every business day) is a business tradition and management standby.

We believe in using a self-help approach as far as practicable; useful resources make self-help work. Realistically, however, there are always times when outside consulting assistance makes sense.

8

Creating a Team Structure to Support System Success

The use of task forces and teams to foster change is familiar to most managers. Teams—indirectly connected to the quality control circles discussed in Chapter 4—provide opportunities for involvement, generate ideas, and help ensure acceptance of change. In a quality management system, work groups automatically become quality teams. The focus of this chapter is on organizing special teams and task forces, identifying quality opportunities, solving problems, developing new or improved methods and procedures, enhancing team processes, and providing recognition for employee and associate contributions.

Organization of Quality Teams and Task Forces

Cross-functional task forces or teams are essential to any broad improvement effort. The reasons are many, and generally clear: improved communication and coordination, improved creativity and generation of ideas, and the motivating impact of involvement. Here are some important actions that management must take when structuring task forces and work teams:

1. Establish the mission.
2. Determine requirements and opportunities to be addressed.
3. Select the leadership or create a protocol for the selection or rotation of leadership.
4. Determine reporting relationships for task force members. Are they full-time or part-time members? Are there multiple supervisory relationships? How will this work?

5. Match membership to the activities to be undertaken.
6. Work through the issue of whether to assign members or ask for volunteers.
7. Define objectives for and with the group at the initial point of contact.
8. Involve membership in task definition.
9. Inventory group-member strengths and weaknesses; provide appropriate quality and group-process training.
10. Delegate responsibilities and authorities; formally empower.
11. Establish a schedule for completing activities; set checkpoints and target dates; clarify accountabilities.
12. Provide resources for the group (e.g., budget, support staff, equipment, and space).

Some of these considerations loom large if an organization is going to embark on team management or self-managing teams. The concept of enabling teams to manage themselves is not new, but applying it extensively in the real world is. Recent estimates are that many U.S. companies are thinking about it. This is an area about which writers put forth lots of articles, with little real experience to back them up. When you read about the hot topic of self-managing teams, be careful. Ask yourself what the writers are *really* saying?

Quality management systems do not require team management, although the approach is clearly consistent with empowerment and other aspects of a sound management system. The material in this chapter is not designed to mandate self-managing teams in your organization, but it is adaptable to team management and will be useful if and when you move in that direction. If a union is present, be sure to consider your obligations under the NLRA.

Exhibit 8-1 is designed to help you determine which aspects of organizing your task forces or teams will require the most effort. Exhibit 8-2 is to be used by task force or team members as a job aid to facilitate their organization and functioning. Management must review the same list to prepare its responses.

Task Force Meetings

What is expected in terms of task force interactions? The model in Exhibit 8-3 shows three meeting variations (but remember that one-on-one contact also builds teamwork and improves communication). The model takes into account frequency and intensity. Frequency is a matter of deciding and then scheduling how often groups need to get together.

Exhibit 8-1. Establishing a task force structure.

Rank the following considerations from 1 (most demanding) to 10 (least demanding) in terms of their challenge in establishing a successful and effective task force structure. Then identify the rank position where the items change from being challenging to *not* challenging (e.g., items 1–6 may be challenging; items 7–10 not). The challenging items will have to be worked on carefully; the others will largely (but never totally) take care of themselves. The first group requires a deliberate approach to managing change (see Chapter 6). Make notes to use in handling the change process and determine which items have a place in your Master Manual.

_____ Establishing the role/purpose for the particular group

_____ Identifying the group's interfaces and how best to manage them

_____ Determining the group's authority(ies) and reporting relationship(s)

_____ Establishing group membership

_____ Fostering teamwork and cooperation internally

_____ Finding the best ways to schedule the group's activities and interactions

_____ Developing the kinds of assignments/responsibilities necessary for members

_____ Integrating the new task force structure with ongoing activities

_____ Finding the best way(s) to resolve the issue of group leadership and group recognition

_____ Identifying the group's priorities (critical, incidental)

Intensity is a matter of preventing the meetings from focusing on interpersonal issues. Outside help in the form of a facilitator may improve the process.

In order to build teamwork and ensure good use of meeting time, there are three qualities that must be present in any meeting framework: focus, structure, and cultural relevance. Focus involves purpose and direction; structure involves organization and resources; and culture involves how things are done in the organization. For task force or team planning purposes, there are quality considerations for each type of task force meeting.

(Text continues on page 152)

Exhibit 8-2. Establishing task force parameters.

The basic question

- What role will the task force (team) play in the organization?

Assumptions

- What assumptions are being made about this activity?
- What limitations realistically exist?
- What do we know for sure about our role? What are our options and opinions?
- What values do we have individually and as a group that relate to our work?
- What do the organization's needs seem to be? What are its leaders' needs? What are the group's needs?

Identification

- What name should we adopt for the quality initiative?
- Should this task force *have* a name?

Purpose

- What is the organization's long-range purpose? What is our purpose as a group?
- What do we want the overall quality initiative to accomplish? What do *we* want to contribute?

Interface(s)

- What other initiatives are under way or being launched that might be related to our work?
- What kind of interface(s) do we need? What interface qualities do we want?
- How will we manage communication, coordination, conflict?

Priorities

- Which of our purposes is absolutely essential (the "musts")?
- Which are important?
- Which are incidental?

Authority/decision making

- What decisions can we make? How?
- What authority exists? How empowered are we?

- What recommendations can the group make, and to whom?
- How will implementation be handled?

Involvement

- Who will be involved with the group? Will some people be involved all the time, some part of the time? What are the decision rules for involvement?
- What will different people or subgroups be asked to do? With what resources?

Objectives for the first time period (e.g., two weeks)

- What steps should we take to get started?
- Which commitments should we make for the first quarter? First year?
- How will we integrate our work with the TQMeeting process in work units?
- What other quality results can be accomplished concurrently?
- Are we being realistic about our program? Have we considered what it takes to make things work and last?
- What are our expectations regarding recognition and reward?

Assignments/responsibilities

- Who will be responsible for doing what within the group? When? With what accountability?
- How much time does each person have to commit?
- Does anyone need special arrangements? Permission?
- Who will take the lead in terms of agendas, facilities, equipment, minutes, reports?

Schedule

- When do we expect to complete the key events in our part of the quality initiative?
- When do we expect to accomplish our other commitments?
- When can we get together?

Tactics

- How do we plan to carry off our role and responsibilities?
- How can we obtain leader and colleague commitment to our inputs?
- How can we gain the organization's support for our actions?
- How will we work with the unions?

(continues)

Exhibit 8-2.   Continued.

Teamwork

- Do we want to adopt a particular team development model (e.g., the three-part model shown in Exhibit 8-3)?
- How will we examine the ways in which we work together?
- What norms do we want operating in our team process?
- When should we measure ourselves on teamwork? Should we consider a facilitator?

Evaluation

- How do we plan to monitor the progress we make in the quality system?
- How will we track our specific quality contributions? How will TQMetrics integrate?
- What, if any, statistical procedures need to be in place?
- What will we do to benchmark our contributions? Our teamwork?
- How do we plan to evaluate our work over time?

Communication Meetings to Exchange Information

Focus: Discussing mission and purpose; reviewing and clarifying organizational objectives; developing an understanding of policies and procedures; reviewing specific quality goals; fitting the Trilogy elements together; becoming up-to-date on emerging quality developments

Structure: Having agendas and schedules; making appropriate physical arrangements and getting necessary materials and resources; having copies of the Master Manual

Culture: Dealing with team leadership; working with shared control; achieving congruence with norms of openness, sharing, and cooperation; ensuring prompt exchange of information

Working Meetings to Problem-Solve and Plan

Focus: Handling quality issues, challenges, and problems; identifying quality project opportunities; pursuing informal group training

Exhibit 8-3. Three-part task force meeting model.

		SCHEDULE	
High	*Every 2 Weeks*	*As Appropriate*	*Semi-annually, Annually*
I			Process/Procedure Meetings
N			
T			
E		Working (Planning,	(Potential Outside
N		Problem-Solving)	Facilitator Zone)
S		Meetings	
I			
T	Communication	(One-to-One	
Y	Meetings	Contact[s])	
Low/high	F R E Q U E N C Y		Low

Structure: Applying the problem-solving or planning model of choice; using delegated authority; providing accountability; applying available data and information; using job aids (see below) effectively

Culture: Identifying appropriate communication channels; facilitating participation and achieving empowerment; tapping into reward systems; clarifying individual roles and relationships; conducting "skunk works" activities

Process or Procedure Meetings

Focus: Fitting in with organizational guidance and preferences as to how group process is used; using task force or team training program content; responding to facilitator suggestions

Structure: Applying information and opinion survey design, processing, and analysis; using interview and focus group activities; applying feedback processes; arranging consulting assistance

Culture: Making recommended changes to facilitate quality progress; identifying and moving in desired new cultural directions; responding to team preferences as to changes in roles and relationships

Exhibit 8-4. Job aid: The problem-solving (planning) model.

[*Note:* Problem solving and planning are similar; planning variations are in parentheses.]

1. Identify desired situation/conditions.
   - Make them specific.
   - Make them clear.
2. Gather the facts: What results need to be achieved? (*Planning:* What is the current situation?)
   - Ask who, what, where, when, how, and how much.
   - Observe the status quo.
3. Define the problem: What has changed? (*Planning:* Define the target: Where do you want to be?)
   - Examine the differences between where you are and where you want to be.
   - Describe the problem (opportunity, challenge) in concrete terms.
4. Look for probable causes: What best explains the change(s)? Examine the driving and restraining forces using the force-field analysis in Exhibit 2-1).
   - Analyze the facts.
   - Consider the involvement of people, data, and things.
5. Develop alternative solutions (*Planning:* identify strategies/tactics).
   - Brainstorm for possibilities or other methods, such as fishbone analysis or nominal group.
   - List, discuss, rank order.
   - Involve others.
6. Choose the alternatives that will restore or establish the desired situation.
   - Evaluate consistency, time, and cost.
   - Consider practicality, acceptability, impact, and implications.
7. Establish steps for implementation.
   - State objectives for restoring or establishing desired situations.
   - Define exactly what you want to accomplish.
   - Develop an action plan.
   - Document actions and responsibilities.
   - List needed resources.
   - Set target dates.
   - Establish evaluation measures.
   - Communicate the decision.
   - Secure understanding and agreement from others.

Job Aids as Self-Help Tools

A job aid is a brief—usually one or two pages—model, checklist, or instrument that presents important and complex information in simple form. The two keys to good job-aid design are a deep understanding of the topic and an ability to highlight and summarize main points. Job aids are essential for self-help approaches to installing systems (see Exhibits 8-4 through 8-8).

Team and Task Force Evaluation

Once your quality teams or task forces have been up and running and are on a six-month schedule, ask yourself these questions to determine their effectiveness:

- How can the quality of your task force or team operations be improved?
- What additional/different resources are needed?
- Do your quality task forces or teams need additional management support? If so, why? How will such support be arranged and structured?
- Is the three-meeting model (a key strategy for team building) working? Is there a need for additional variations? Will the suggested schedule work? If not, what changes are needed?
- Many team-building experts think that focus and structure are easiest to handle and that process or procedure is tougher in terms of team willingness to tackle interactions. Does this fit your experience? When do you think a facilitator helps? Why?
- Does your task force or team need special training on group process methods? If so, which ones? How can this be handled?
- Can you determine whether the organization's quality task force or team members are functioning effectively with one another? How?
- Are participants in task force and team activities and processes being appropriately recognized and rewarded?
- How would you react if a senior executive at your location said, "This group stuff is a waste of time; give me managers who can make decisions"? What implications do you see for using a task force strategy to enhance quality initiatives?
- Job aids have grown in popularity, particularly the tightly organized or "one-pager" kind. Is your organization using job aids

(Text continues on page 159)

Exhibit 8-5. Job aid: The fishbone model.

There are numerous methods for solving problems. Graphic approaches are helpful to those who work better when they can see a picture of the issues. A "fishbone" diagram is one such tool; not surprisingly, it takes the form of the skeleton of a fish. Credit for the fishbone approach is given to Kaoru Ishikawa. Here is a graphic example:

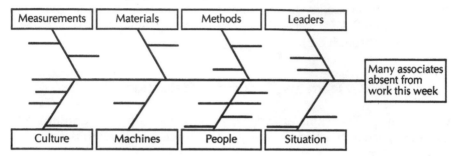

The fishbone approach involves six steps:

1. Define the problem as clearly as possible; be prepared to redefine it as more relevant information is uncovered. Defining a problem is almost always an iterative process.
2. Write the problem in the briefest possible terms on the right of the diagram, at the end of the arrow line. If a formal statement is needed, write it under the diagram.
3. Brainstorm broad areas that might contain the cause of the problem. A model of the usual elements involved (e.g., materials, machines, methods, labor) or a creativity checklist may stimulate thinking. The problem may defy specification until sufficient specifics are added to clarify what is going on.
4. Given the available information, place specifics (potential causes, subcauses) in the diagram as branches and bones.
5. Select the few conditions or activities that are most likely causes; elaborate these with additional details (more fishbones). The statistical analog is a Pareto diagram in which the most prevalent condition is identified, followed by those less prevalent, in order of occurrence. Pareto had this statistical concept: Develop the percentage represented by various possible causes of problems, and array them in order, worst to least, for emphasis. Work the worst first.
6. Verify the correctness and seriousness of the cause(s) selected; identify and develop solutions as with any other problem-solving process (e.g., identify alternatives, weigh and evaluate, select the best).

The Fishbone diagram has become one of the basic quality tools. It is totally adaptable for working on management problems.

Exhibit 8-6.   Job aid: Enhancing creativity—a checklist approach.

Creativity is crucial to planning and solving problems. Imagination should be used at every step of the problem-solving process, but ideas may not flow easily. A checklist can prove useful, although a creativity checklist seems almost to be a contradiction in terms.

Ask yourself questions such as these if you need inspiration as you apply the steps of problem solving (planning):

Adaptation

- What else is like this?
- What ideas does this suggest?
- What else could be adapted to this purpose?
- What models can be followed?
- What can be imitated?
- What analogies or metaphors can be used for perspective?

Modification

- What if this were changed?
- How could it be made better?
- What change could be made in the process?
- What change could be made in the results?
- In what other form or guise could this appear?
- In what other package could it appear?

Substitution

- What can be used instead of this?
- What other ingredient or part could be used?
- What other process could be used?
- Who else could be involved?
- Where else could this take place?

Addition

- What can be added?
- Should this be stronger, better, bigger, or faster?
- What extra value can be added to this?
- What other features can be added?

(continues)

Exhibit 8-6.   Continued.

Subtraction

- What can be subtracted?
- Should this be smaller, weaker, slower, or more compact?
- Can it be compressed or compacted?
- Can miniatures or smaller versions be used?

Multiplication

- What if this were magnified?
- What if it were doubled or quadrupled?
- What if it were overstated?
- What is the extreme version?

Division

- What if this were split up into fewer parts?
- Could it be done with fewer parts?
- What if certain parts were left out?

Rearrangement

- How else could this be arranged?
- What if the order were changed?
- What other layout could be used?
- Could it be rearranged physically?

Sequence

- What other schedule could be used?
- Could the timing of events be changed?
- What should come after what?
- What should come first, and what last?

Reversal

- What if this were backwards?
- What if positive were negative, or good were bad?
- What if it were turned upside down, or turned around?
- What if roles were reversed?

Combination

- What ideas, processes, or events can be combined?
- What combinations, blends, assortments, or ensembles could be used?
- What if things were merged or clustered?

---

for task force or team members? If so, do you need to make improvements? If not, would you like to?
- The "bottom-line" question: Can you see progress in quality because of task force or team initiatives? If so, why? If not, why not?

Improvement of Task Force and Team Functioning

Congruent with the philosophy of continuous improvement, quality task forces and teams have an obligation to assess their performance and institute needed changes in their process and results. Exhibit 8–8 provides an instrument designed to achieve this purpose. The instrument should be used on a scheduled and as-needed basis. The as-needed use can be proposed by any member at any time to respond to a situation perceived as less than fully effective.

Use the following questions to build on your group strengths and eliminate weaknesses. Ask the questions periodically.

- What are your major strengths as a group?
- What are your major weaknesses?
- What major problems and opportunities will your group face in the next few months? The next year?
- What actions will be taken to build on the group's strengths and compensate for its weaknesses (what to keep, get rid of, or change)? Specify in terms of quality objectives or goals.
- When and by whom will these actions be taken?
- When and how will your group receive feedback on its progress toward improved effectiveness?

Summary

Most quality programs rely on task forces and teams to bring a unique and useful contribution to quality initiatives. But without proper orga-

(Text continues on page 163)

Exhibit 8-7. Job aid: Group process techniques—developing consensus.

Guidelines

• Avoid arguing for your own solution. Present your position as clearly and logically as possible. Consider seriously the reactions of others.

• Avoid "win-lose" stalemates in discussing solutions. If an impasse occurs, look for another alternative acceptable to those involved.

• Avoid changing your mind *only* to avoid conflict and reach agreement and harmony. Don't yield when another view appears to have a logical foundation *if* you have good reason to question it. Be flexible and reasonable, but don't accept something that makes no sense to you. Probe.

• Avoid conflict-reducing techniques such as votes, averaging, splitting the difference, bargaining, and coin flipping. Differences of opinion often indicate incomplete discussion or inadequate information. As chairperson, be intolerant of unilateral action, railroading by a few, or abdication of responsibility by the group in favor of one or two members.

• View differences of opinion as natural and helpful rather than as a hindrance in decision making. Generally, the more ideas expressed the greater the likelihood of conflict, but the richer the array of resources.

• View any quick initial agreement as suspect. Probe the reasons underlying quick agreements. Before incorporating them as group decisions, make sure that people have reached a similar solution for the same basic reasons or for complimentary reasons.

Brainstorming

Brainstorming is used to generate ideas in problem solving or planning. It helps stimulate and capture creative inputs that might otherwise not be generated or considered. Here are some useful ground rules for a brainstorming session:

• Rule out criticism. Withhold judgment, analysis, or evaluation until after the session has ended.

• Think freely. Accept "wild" ideas.

• Encourage quantity; maintain a rapid pace. The objective is the maximum number of ideas in the time available.

• Build on other ideas. Seek combinations, embellishments, and improvements.

• Allow enough time when setting up the meeting. Announce the meeting's purpose and topic so that the participants can do some advance thinking.

• Continue until the flow of ideas runs dry. Restimulate the flow at least once by referring to points previously made. If the brainstorming is still going well when the scheduled meeting time is up, extend the session on the spot or reconvene the group as soon as practicable.

• Note key ideas. Use a flipchart (easel, pad) or chalkboard.

• As leader, bring participants in if they seem to be holding back.

• Clarify ideas, but try not to interrupt the flow of ideas. One participant's contribution can trigger another's ideas.

• Use a creativity checklist (see Exhibit 8-6) to stimulate creative ideas.

• Plan for evaluation at the end of the session, when the best ideas will be chosen. Consider which ideas are practical or doable (e.g., timing, simplicity, cost, consistency, acceptability, endurance) and which ideas are useful and will help improve the organization (e.g., achieve objectives, increase effectiveness, reduce obstacles).

• Recognize that evaluation and choice may involve further combining or embellishing of ideas previously suggested. It may be the second part of the brainstorming itself, or it may take place soon after (e.g., after a break). The leader could work with the brainstorming results without the input of participants, but this is not usually the best use of the group's talents and skills.

The Nominal Group Technique

More structured and rigid than brainstorming, the nominal group approach involves the following:

• Participants are organized into groups of eight to fifteen people.

• The problem, issue, or opportunity is stated.

• For five to fifteen minutes, individuals silently and independently write down all their ideas (have pads and pencils available).

• Each individual presents one of his or her best ideas to the group without discussion. Ideas are presented to the group on a round-robin basis and are recorded and numbered on a flipchart in summary form.

• Group members exchange information to clarify content. Individuals respond to questions, and connections are developed.

• Individuals determine the rank order (top five, bottom five) or rating of those ideas recorded silently.

• Priorities are established through the pooled outcome of individual votes.

• The group analyzes the highest-valued contributions.

• The group reaches agreement or reranks and reanalyzes top items.

Exhibit 8-8.   Job aid: Assessing team effectiveness.

Below are some statements that describe possible reactions to your group meetings. Decide whether you have these reactions almost always, often, sometimes, seldom, or almost never.

1. Almost never
2. Seldom
3. Sometimes
4. Often
5. Almost always

1. I am using my time well when I attend a team meeting.
   1 2 3 4 5
2. Team members do a good job of handling disagrements.
   1 2 3 4 5
3. I am able to make a good contribution to the team.
   1 2 3 4 5
4. Team members communicate frankly and openly with one another. 1 2 3 4 5
5. I am committed to the agreements we come to in our meetings. 1 2 3 4 5
6. Team members have trust and confidence in one another.
   1 2 3 4 5
7. I am able to be creative and do not have to watch my every word at meetings. 1 2 3 4 5
8. Team members talk to the whole team and do not form cliques.
   1 2 3 4 5
9. I am able to get enough time in a meeting to say what I have to say. 1 2 3 4 5
10. Team members are all interested in what goes on.
    1 2 3 4 5
11. I am sure that everyone in the team gets a good chance to be heard. 1 2 3 4 5
12. Team members support one another and build on the ideas of others. 1 2 3 4 5
13. I am sure that we reach agreement on the basis of a team consensus. 1 2 3 4 5
14. Team members listen carefully and do not prejudge what others say. 1 2 3 4 5
15. I know that my opinions are wanted by other team members. 1 2 3 4 5

16. Team members feel good about their involvement and participation. 1 2 3 4 5
17. I feel responsible for helping achieve what the team agrees to do. 1 2 3 4 5
18. Team members are more productive as a result of getting together. 1 2 3 4 5
19. I believe that my work with the team positively impacts our organization'a qualify performance. 1 2 3 4 5
20. Team members are committed as a group to continuous quality improvement and work hard for it. 1 2 3 4 5

My score: _____

In which items (pick up to three) would you most like to see improvement?

_____   _____   _____

A local approach to scoring and discussion should be arranged. One easy method is to have team members complete two copies of the questionnaire. One is placed anonymously in a central collection place; a volunteer runs the averages by item and distributes a master copy. The team meets to discuss improvement potential. This fits the procedure meeting element of the team process model; in many situations, facilitator assistance will improve the results of the discussion.

---

nization and attention to leadership issues, teams can lose direction and momentum; they will not function without management recognition and support. The role of maintaining the team structure must be created, assigned, and monitored.

Task forces and teams need expertise in order to function. This means exposure to quality training at some level (see Chapter 5 and Appendix B); it may mean more-intensified and -specialized team training. The Japanese have been successful with quality circles partly because of their willingness to make a substantial training investment. Although this may seem to make economic sense amortized over a lifetime of employment, the real reason it makes sense is that it pays off for the organization. The trick is to do the right training in the right way and not squander time and money on irrelevant investments.

Job aids are extremely helpful to the successful functioning of task forces and teams. And task forces and teams should engage in a continuous quality improvement process of their own, using measurement, feedback, and tracking.

9

Developing System Implementation Tools: The Triad

Much of this chapter on implementation and operation connects with the earlier chapters, particularly those having to do with the system launch. It is designed to be the linchpin for the formation of your total management quality system.

The Operations Phase

There are two parts in the operations phase. Part 1 involves creating a simple three-part paper-and-pencil system that gets people comfortable with the quality management system model as a way of running the business. The heart of the system, the TQ Triad, is tailored locally, using relevant models, forms, checklists, inventories, measurements, and the like. Later, it can be switched to a fully automated or embedded computer system. This is a pivotal point in the creation of your quality management system.

Part 1 of the Operations Phase

It is time to plan the preliminary steps needed to carry out part 1 of the operations phase. These following steps must occur.

1. Communicate program objectives on a broad-scale basis.
2. Organize quality task forces or teams, training them as necessary.

3. Conduct QMS training as necessary.*
4. Introduce part 1 of the operations phase at lower levels:
   —Use additional assessment instruments; have lower levels and field locations benchmark processes, and provide direction for local activities.
   —Communicate the quality management system model, Master Manual, and related concepts; discuss ISO 9000 or Baldrige Award intentions with or without time lines.
   —Provide clear overall direction; describe specific job aids and other materials that will be provided.
   —Undertake special organizational efforts to identify useful, acceptable "metrics." This is a major issue, because any existing metrics must be able to become the "base case" or be adjusted or replaced for best use of measurement.
5. Identify by name and by organization those who will take the lead in the initial system activities.
6. Notify those who are to be responsible and obtain their input before taking any further steps. Gather these key people at a meeting.
7. Publish the action plan.
8. Finally, fund and otherwise resource the needed activities and obtain agreement on initial objectives and time lines.

If part 1 is well planned and the organization sticks with the plan, it will be relatively easy to move the quality management system into part 2. The seam may be invisible.

Part 2 of the Operations Phase

Part 2 involves the adoption of tougher changes, such as new human resources management approaches and more challenging measurement and reporting processes; it may involve announcement of an intention to become certified under ISO 9000 or to compete for the Baldrige Award.

Caution: Total management quality installations won't work on a lockstep basis; each location has to be comfortable with its approach. Rigid overemphasis on methods and procedures will kill creativity and destroy the use of common sense. Most disappointments or failures come from micromanaging, and especially from micromanaging quality initiatives. Any management system is a mistake if it leads to a special-

---

* Appendix B has a complete manager/supervisor and employee/associate curriculum; it should be used to refine training needs, and potential action steps.

ized, large, expensive organization; excessive reviews; activities that do not clearly contribute to progress; unnecessary training; and, perhaps worst of all, quotas.

Early Questions

As you take the first steps toward implementing your quality management system, here are some things to think about:

- How can you most effectively create a bridge from the work that has gone into the Master Manual to the TQ Triad?
- The preparation and launch activities generated significant information about your organization's present state with respect to quality system readiness and potential challenges. How can you make best use of the data?
- Is there a part of the organization that should be considered to pilot the key concepts of the quality management system? What considerations would go into your choice?
- Who can best accept responsibility for turning out the publications of the TQ Triad? How many copies of each element will you need, given a probable shelf life of three years?
- What experience have you had with organizational changes that rely extensively on ad hoc groups (e.g., task forces) to carry out important responsibilities? Was the experience positive or negative? What are the consequences today?

TQ Triad Specifics

TQManagement

TQManagement (see Exhibit 9-1) is a thirty- to thirty-five–page publication containing the vision, philosophy, and direction of the quality management system. It illustrates the models, tools, and techniques of quality and productivity improvement. It supports the activities of employees and associates at all levels and in all specialties. TQManagement should be a stand-alone publication that can be shared with other organizations.

TQManagement incorporates up-to-date quality concepts so as to avoid committing immediately to Baldrige Award participation, unless and until the organization decides to go forward. Every step the organization takes, however, can be completely congruent with Award Guidelines and appropriately documented.

TQMetrics

TQMetrics (see Exhibits 9-2 and 9-3) consists of ten to fifteen pages of introduction, forms, checklists, and schedules that identify objectives and measures, track progress, and enable evaluations to be performed. The content may need to be tailored for major functions and departments; the example in Exhibit 9-3 has been designed to be as neutral as possible. The target is the installation of a sound management system first, with specific quality assignments added as a natural next step. Each employee has a personal version of the notebook (a log); managers have a personal version plus a composite for the organization, which would probably contain summarized rather than original data. There is a direct tie between the Master Manual content and TQMetrics. TQMetrics is a major tool for bringing to fruition the desired situation described and targeted in the Master Manual.

The measurements involved may be related to both individual responsibilities and/or commitments with respect to continuous improvement and contributions to department (and higher) management and quality objectives. This logging approach works. It focuses attention and motivates desired performance. It provides a solid basis for recognizing contributions.

Periodically, employees and associates get together in a task force or team setting to discuss progress and adjust commitments (see the following discussion on TQMeetings as well as Chapter 8). TQMetrics functions as the source document. Task force or team leaders (or volunteer members) aggregate ideas and data, as appropriate, to pass them up the ladder. If the group is not a natural work group, data from a variety of sources will have to be aggregated and integrated to create an effective communication.

All information channeled up must be acknowledged. It is essential that the organization have a standard operating procedure for responding to quality improvement communications and that the time frame allow for provision of feedback. Recognition and reward are fundamental to continuing success.

Some informal training in the mechanics of using the logging system may be appropriate; this would be part of the initial team TQMeeting. With experienced managers and supervisors coaching employees, this activity may not require much support.

TQMeetings

Provide half-day to one-and-a-half–day working meetings (with a focus on communication, planning, training, and procedure) to *introduce*

(Text continues on page 175)

Exhibit 9-1.   TQManagement outline.

Chapter 1

Introduction to the total quality management system; statement of vision/purpose; understanding the relationship to TQM systems; economic demands and opportunities; key definition(s); relationship to previous approaches.

Chapter 2

Organizational performance concepts: quality management vision; specific organizational targets; quality system leadership; project or activity selection, sponsorship, and stewardship; customer concepts (internal, external); continuous improvement approaches; statistical quality control concepts; benchmarking mechanisms; vertical/horizontal performance improvement approaches:

• *Vertical.* More intense management (the historical strategy; opportunities are largely exhausted); not much potential for improvement left unless one goes after a full reengineering of the organization

• *Horizontal.* Task force and work team organization for quality management (the fundamental management quality strategy; team management potential; mission statements and objectives; documentation of activities, minutes; action plans; communication channels and approvals; accessing resources; inter- and intraorganizational arrangements; cross-functional mechanisms; task force leadership and membership; new communication and coordination initiatives; enhanced involvement in planning and problem solving; specialized training; group process approaches to assist task force and team activities; access to process facilitators; reports and recommendations)

Chapter 3

Operation of the two-part operations system:

• *Part 1.* TQMetrics and TQMeetings installations; pilot approach(es); Master Manual integration; statistical quality control (SQC) integration, procedural preferences, and examples; change in management considerations; communication and training delivery approaches; installation of stewardship and review mechanics; recognition opportunities; "Evergreen" litmus test(s)

• *Part 2.* As above, expanded and refined; application of learnings from pilots as appropriate

Chapter 4

Dimensions to be influenced in the TQMeeting process:

- Continuous improvement of quality management procedures and quality practices
- Choice of optimum standards and measures for task force/team use; continual testing of usefulness
- Analysis of effectiveness of organizational culture and customs (including leadership effectiveness and human resources involvement and empowerment)

Chapter 5

Examples of degrees of freedom for task forces and work teams:

- Methods and work flow optimization (flowcharts for analyzing and benchmarking performance progress)
- Organization and work design
- Time management (as an organizational issue)
- Staffing management (right people at right place and time)
- Others (as selected or directed)

Chapter 6

Identify best approach(es):

How task forces and work teams can select the best or most relevant management process improvement approaches for the specific situation; selection based on training and/or staff assistance, including an example of a process model:

Value Analysis

1. Decide appropriate personnel involvement.
2. Identify processes, activities, objectives, and controls available.
3. Identify tasks.
4. Produce work or flowcharts of processes, activities, and/or tasks.
5. Analyze (on a task force or team level):
   - Reengineering checklist/flowcharts: ergonomics, measurement, controls
   - Behavioral checklists/flowcharts: work design, commitment

(continues)

Exhibit 9-1.   Continued.

---

6. Identify priorities for improvement, appropriate metrics, self-measurement (value of own contribution).
7. Develop improvement ideas (on a task force or team basis):
   • Reengineering checklist/model review(s)
   • Enrichment/empowerment
   • Enlargement/rotation
   • Team management (self-managing approach)
8. Prepare action plan(s); review:
   • Communication, coordination
   • Commitment
   • Training, coaching
   • Tracking (self-measurement)
   • Evergreen analysis
9. Implement, document, provide recognition.
10. Obtain feedback; validate or recycle.

Chapter 7

Getting the job done—typical group methods (see Exhibit 8-7):

• Developing consensus
• Brainstorming methods
• Nominal group steps
• Job aid use (provide samples):
   —Problem-solving and planning models
   —Creativity checklist
   —Review of statistical methods
   —Control chart model(s)

Chapter 8

Feedback methods/applications

Chapter 9

Summary

Chapter 10

References

Exhibit 9-2. TQMetrics outline.

Section 1

Introduction: Organization's reputation for excellence and ambition for further improvements to a world-class level; recognition of successful on-going activities; generalized need for new/adjusted management and quality processes; relation to existing statistical quality control technology; expansion of quality concepts to creation of an overall quality management system

---

Section 2

Philosophy (reinforce main points in TQManagement): Proactive response to economic challenges; empowerment; customer needs, performance improvement expectations (internal, external); importance of an Evergreen approach; other (tailored for organization)

Section 3

Essential activities: TQManagement guide describes overall situation (quality, productivity, and accountability assessments) and provides content input (see Exhibit 9-1 for chapter-by-chapter outline).

Section 4

Practical metrics (see Exhibit 9-3): Measurement and evaluation concepts and methods (integrate statistical controls, special process control applications, etc.); measurement design and decision mechanisms and employee/associate involvement; documentation (logging) of improvement ideas and self-measurements (those for which accountable); procedures for stewardship

---

Section 5

Evergreen implications: Measurement reviews; adjustments; recycling

---

Section 6

Task force/quality team operations: Relate use of TQMetrics to three-element meeting model (communication, problem solving/planning, and process/procedure) in Chapter 8.

Section 7

References

Exhibit 9-3.   Sample TQMetrics task force/team measurement and tracking system.

This form is designed to supplement the Master Manual and its tracking sheets and provide a bridge to the TQMetrics concept.

Task force/quality team: _____

Date: _____

   Section 1: Measurement Analysis

   Master Manual tracking sheet (number): _____

   Item description: _____

   Relevant objective(s): _____

   _____

   Expected result(s): _____

   _____

   _____

   _____

   Measurement/metrics procedure(s)—specify the statistic(s) of choice, if

   applicable: _____

   _____

   _____

   _____

   _____

   _____

   Way(s) in which measurement/metrics procedures will be handled:

   _____

   _____

   _____

   _____

   _____

How measurement/metrics findings will be used: _____

_____

_____

_____

_____

Section 2: Developing a Measures/Metrics Worksheet

Current date _____ Next review date _____ Ending date _____

Measurement/metrics specifics (refer to Master Manual tracking sheets):

Type of measure, specific measures selected, success criteria:

_____

_____

_____

Observation Measures

- Competencies (knowledge, skill)
- Motivation to contribute
- Creativity
- Design/manufacturing teamwork
- Environmental concern
- Other: _____

Effectiveness Measures

- Operational result(s)
- Financial progress
- Time utilization/JIT
- Customer response(s)
- Error/defect rates
- Training attendance
- Innovation
- Other: _____

Performance Indicators

- Sales
- Cost of product or service

(continues)

Exhibit 9-3. Continued.

- Quality cost reduction(s)
- Increased service factor(s)
- Handling waste
- Training completed
- Proactive suggestions
- On-time delivery
- Other: _____

Volume Indicators

- Quality suggestions
- Throughput improvement(s)
- Shipping performance
- Complaint reduction(s)
- Adjustments performed
- Other: _____

Section 3: Tracking and Evaluation

Current date _____Next review date _____

Tools Used

- Evidence That Establishes Target Achievement
- Results to Date
- Remediation Needed, Follow-Up
- Individual/Team Responsibility

Observation Measures: _____

_____

Effectiveness Measures: _____

_____

Performance Measures: _____

_____

Volume Indicators: _____

_____

TQManagement, TQMetrics, and *follow-on* TQMeetings to ensure their successful implementation and maintenance (see Chapter 8 for a model, schedule, and job aids).

The work team or natural work unit is the basic quality organization; special quality task forces and quality teams create horizontal bridges and vertical links and supply any needed matrix approaches. We assume that like most organizations, yours is still basically hierarchically organized. Thus, it would be natural to design different introductory TQMeetings for different levels. But if you are experienced in using team management approaches, a unified design for all levels enhances existing teamwork and interface relationships.

If the organization is hierarchical, bring people together by vertical level or role: management, professional/technical, and office/clerical. Work toward team management applications (see Exhibit 9-4 for an approach to curriculum design). If the organization is team-managed, bring vertical and horizontal slices of people together at the same time in keeping with the overall quality system design.

As the quality management system is defined and becomes "how we work around here," work teams will get together for TQMeetings at least biweekly (see Chapter 8). Task forces will operate on an "as needed" basis.

To provide structure (and variety), a process model, such as value analysis (see Exhibit 9-1) or nominal group technique (see Exhibit 8-7), can be suggested for use on a rotating schedule. In effect, working through the model and a timely opportunity or problem become the agenda for the TQMeeting.

A variation of TQMeeting is a two-tier approach to involvement deep in the organization. The first tier involves the rollout phase in which a series of "working meetings" introduces all quality management system activities. The second tier involves a series of ongoing, periodic working meetings (probably biweekly) that keep the quality management system going on an Evergreen basis. The nature of the various working meetings changes with the location and attendees: A problem-solving TQMeeting at headquarters would be different from one at a field location. The agendas would vary, as would the focus of the discussions.

Formal staff support for the TQMeeting process should be available to carry ideas and comments forward, obtain needed information, and facilitate follow-up. There is nothing inherent in the process that will cause it to run itself; it requires the same kind of support and maintenance that is essential in similar team initiatives.

Exhibit 9-4. TQMeetings start-up approach.

Management Working Meeting (Day and a Half)

1. Agree on philosophy, issues, opportunities, methods, and approaches.
2. Transform management considerations.
3. Develop, analyze, and discuss local case situation(s).
4. Learn how to use new system tools (TQManagement, TQMetrics, TQMeetings):
   • Content presentation
   • Intended use(s)
5. Outline an action plan:
   • Goals, time line(s)
   • Metrics
   • Accountabilities

Professional/Technical Working Meeting (One Day)

1. Agree on philosophy, issues, opportunities, approaches.
2. Develop, analyze, and discuss local case situation(s).
3. Learn how to use new system tools (TQManagement, TQMetrics TQMeetings):
4. Outline an action plan
   • Goals, time line(s)
   • Metrics
   • Accountabilities

Office/Clerical Working Meeting (Half-Day)

1. Agree on philosophy, issues, opportunities, approaches.
2. Learn how to use new system tools (TQManagement—selected parts; TQMetrics—all; TQMeetings—selected parts):
   • Content presentation
   • Intended uses
3. Outline an action plan:
   • Goals, time line(s)
   • Metrics
   • Accountabilities

Exhibit 9-5. Summary of system operation.

Management Level	Launch	System Operation		
		Quarterly	Annually	Ongoing
Quality Ranking (Chapter 2 and Exhibit 2-1)	x		x	
Quality Inventory (Chapter 2 and Exhibit 2-1)	x		x	
—Leadership —Information and Analysis —Strategic Quality Planning —Human Resource Development and Management —Management of Process Quality —Quality and Operational Results —Customer Focus and Satisfaction				
Senior Executive Offsite(s)	x	x		
Supervisor/Manager Training	x			x
Employee/Associate Training	x			x
Communication Plan/Action	x			x
Benchmarking	x			x
Evergreen Plan/Action	x			x

*Extend downward through the organization for process benchmarking, progress measurement. This provides direction to much of the overall quality management process, and emulates MBNQA scoring.

All Employee/Associate Level	System Operation			
	Daily/Weekly	Quarterly	Annually	Ongoing
TQM Inventory (Chapter 2)*			x	
—Leadership —Information and Analysis				

(continues)

Exhibit 9-5.   Continued.

All Employee/Associate Level	System Operation			
	Daily/Weekly	Quarterly	Annually	Ongoing
—Strategic Quality Planning				
—Human Resource Development and Management				
—Management of Process Quality				
—Quality and Operational Results				
—Customer Focus and Satisfaction				
TQMetrics—Personal/ Team Objectives/ Measures (Part 1)	x	x		
TQMetrics—Personal/ Team Objectives/ Measures (Part 2)	x	x		
TQMeetings (Work Group; Parts 1 and 2)		x		
—Methods/Work Flow Optimization				
—Organization/Job/ Work Design				
—Staffing				
—Time Utilization				
—Other(s)				
TQManagement Improvements (Parts 1 and 2; open channel communication for QMS model improvements; all employees; special scheduled TQMeetings for senior leaders; follows follow-on use of the TQM Inventory)		x		x

All Employee/Associate Level	System Operation			
	Daily/Weekly	*Quarterly*	*Annually*	*Ongoing*
—Leadership				
—Information and Analysis				
—Strategic Quality Planning				
—Human Resource Development and Management				
—Management of Process Quality				
—Quality Performance and Results				
—Customer Focus and Satisfaction				

*Provides direction to overall quality management system improvement initiatives; emulates MBNQA scoring.

Summary

The total management quality system that operates with the tools of the TQ Triad is simple and easy to handle. It is an excellent vehicle for managers who want a clear picture of where they are going and how to get there. With periodic evaluation and fine-tuning of the system, the organization can build and maintain an effective, custom-made management system (see Exhibit 9-5).

1. *TQManagement* is a mechanism for communicating understanding, relating the Master Manual concept to system implementation, and a protocol for resolving role obligations and resource allocation conflicts.
2. *TQMetrics* provides a way for the quality system to "travel" with employees/associates and take advantage of the motivational power of self-measurement; it facilitates making notes of ideas, and is the formal mechanism for tracking measurements for which the employee/associate has responsibility.
3. *TQMeetings* is a flexible, straightforward process for facilitating the working together of groups toward any objective—in this case quality management.

Success in implementing new or expanded systems accompanies logical and careful introductions. When the rollout begins, pilot programs help; phasing is almost essential. Once the system rollout has begun, it will become clear where conflict exists between the organizational culture and the system values and mechanics. The organization must be prepared to return to managing change and the Evergreen Process at any time (see Chapter 11).

Part Four

Getting Premium Performance From Your Quality Management System

This last part is as important, if not more important, than much of what has gone before. Why? Because more management initiatives fail by reason of ignoring lessons gleaned from pilot programs and launch activities, neglecting to measure and assess progress, paying inadequate attention to feedback, and allowing indicated adjustments to slip than for lack of front-end planning activity. Lots of people plan well; the more creative the person, the more fun planning is. But in many settings, there is little or no accountability for plans; they can be changed or set aside almost on a whim.

Once substantial resources are committed and consumed, the situation changes significantly. Once operations begin, results must then be stewarded. This is the point when significant learning, and perhaps even greater progress than anticipated, becomes available if—and that's a big *if*—the people involved really put an effort into fine-tuning operations based on their own experience and experience gleaned from others. To do this well means considering the desired key results at the operation's design phase, not after the fact. This is why Evergreen System elements must be built in to the management system at the beginning.

Measurement, Feedback, and Benchmarking

Fundamental to ongoing success are periodic measurement of results and feedback of the measurements to those involved. Understanding and ownership are maximized when people work on their own measurements and perform their own interpretations (TQMetrics) and follow by planning for additional and expanded progress. The likelihood of future improvements increases when commitments become public, as is the case when a team gets together to critique its operation and establish new or revised objectives.

Most of Chapter 10 is devoted to feedback, its acquisition and its application. Feedback feeds into benchmarking (already discussed in Chapter 6). Having benchmarks to rely on has always been critical. Think of how crazy a soccer or a football game would be without yard lines and goals! But in many business operations, the idea of benchmarking, especially with another organization in the same industry, is discouraged. True, human resources people share information all the time in the form of wage and salary surveys and opinion survey databases, but this is an exception. After all, federal legislation frowns upon competitors sharing operational information for such purposes as gaining control of a market. Without carrying logic too far, some of the ills of U.S. industry might well have been avoided if there had been a tradition of sharing rather than isolation. Today there is a new appreciation of the importance of benchmarking as a key quality management tool. This mandates leaders' awareness of its importance and applications and an ability to take action to introduce it on both an internal and external basis.

Leadership

Leaders must be able to come back with more when an initiative starts to sag. It is virtually impossible to avoid having a system run down over time. People change, and enthusiasm changes with them. They get bored, and what was once important simply blends in with the paint on the wall. Leaders must stay in touch with what is going on, push hard for progress, confront disappointments, build pride, provide rewards, and make periodic adjustments to the details. The leader's role is to step up activity and perhaps take personal control; otherwise, they are likely to lose the battle.

Assessment and recycling are not the end of the systems management model; they are a continuous contributor to improvement in the finest traditions of general and quality management.

Evergreen

Chapter 11 is where you will learn about the Evergreen process in detail—how to sustain and enhance your new system. Failure to apply the concepts in Chapters 10 and 11 is precisely why 70 percent of the quality initiatives fail.

10

Going Operational and Getting Feedback

You have thought through creating a team structure (Chapter 8) and examined ways to construct your own tailored Triad (Chapter 9). Now is the time to consider what you want to do to optimize a full operational process and obtain feedback. Here are some questions to ask:

• *How can you capture and use the experience gained in the pilot activities that were part of your launch phase?* How can experiences be evaluated and disseminated so that the rest of the organization can benefit? Do you have a plan to go wall-to-wall with your quality management system? Who are the leaders? How can you continue to demonstrate your commitment?

• *Do you need additional off-site meetings as you cascade the process down and across the organization?* Who should conduct the sessions? Who should attend? What materials are needed? How should objective/goal setting be handled? What success stories can be highlighted?

• *What has to be done to optimize the Master Manual approach?* Are there changes that should be made? Are the metrics of choice holding up? Can you build up the manuals that have been created by level and organizational element by scanning the Trilogy again and picking up items previously designated for later inclusion?

• *Does the material in the Triad (TQManagement, TQMetrics, TQMeetings) need revision?* What do you have to do to get the final versions printed and distributed?

• *What have your experiences been with suppliers and customers, both internal and external?* Has your activity been communicated to other companies to which you provide products or services? Have you satisfied customer requirements as a preferred vendor? Do your employees and associates know who their customers are? Do they know what they need and their level of expectations? Have they been able to quantify customer requirements in terms of quantity, quality, cost, and timeliness?

• *How are you doing with empowerment?* Have you expanded delegation to employees and associates? Do you need to equip them further to accept increased authority and responsibility? How are task forces and work teams handling empowerment? Are people eager to "take the bit in their teeth"? If not, what is getting in the way? Think about your organizational culture; is it compatible with your values, aims, and objectives?

• *Do you see policies and procedures that should be changed?* What changes in management philosophy or personnel are indicated? What "force field" analyses should be conducted? Have the changes affected employees' view of the organization as a good place to work? Has anyone left because of the new environment? Do you see people who are resistant to the point of being obstreperous? What do you need to do about them?

• *In the human resources management area, what attention needs to be paid to your performance management system (objective setting, performance appraisal, feedback, compensation)?* Do you need to investigate gain sharing? Do you need to change or expand your recognition practices? How were the rewards associated with the launch and pilot program(s) received? What are the collective bargaining implications? How is the union responding to the new initiatives? Can you hire the kind of person you need to optimize your new organization?

• *What steps and schedules need to be established to introduce managers, professionals, and other employees to your total management quality system.*

• *How can new deployment areas be added? What is the logical progression?* Is there a need for phasing? If so, what is the optimum sequence?

• *Can you now be fairly specific about time lines?* When should things happen? How long should it be before they take hold?

• *What expanded communication activities are indicated?* What messages need to be sent to employees and associates? Which channels will work best? What media will be best? Who should speak to the organization?

• *What next steps, if any, are appropriate for training?* Is any training needed? What did you learn from the system training during the pilots? How will you organize the system training for other groups? Can you integrate specialized quality system training into ongoing training activities? Can people handle the metrics involved in your system? Are task forces effective in their interactions? Do work teams continue to work effectively given the new initiatives?

• *Have you identified areas for benchmarking?* Have you identified potential benchmarking partners? Have you become familiar with the American Productivity and Quality Center's International Benchmarking Clearinghouse? Do you know about other services for specialized functions (e.g., Society for Human Resource Management/Saratoga Institute effectiveness program)? If you used an organizational assessment survey, is it time to run it again? Is it time to use it more broadly in the organization?

• *Have you given any thought to ISO 9000 registration?* How about competing for the Baldrige Award? What steps do you need to take to move forward?

Obtaining and Evaluating Feedback

Feedback has always been important to the operation of a management system. You need feedback from your launch and pilot program activities, as should be clear from the series of questions posed above.

As a term, *feedback* is used in several ways. On an individual basis, feedback generally refers to one person giving another person some insight into how the second person's behavior is seen. A classic example is the information a supervisor provides about an employee's or associate's work performance: "Sam, you've suddenly developed a pattern of delivering one less order per day than we had agreed on. Will you help me understand what's going on?" Or: "Joan, you're doing a terrific job with the new quality reports. They're on time, complete, and accurate. Getting such a great start on a new system is really important. Let me know if there's something we can pass on to other groups. Keep up the good work!"

Feedback serves the purpose of positioning the individual's situation, obtaining information about what is happening, and enabling recognition (or providing a basis for discipline). Without feedback, things just don't run as well as they should. Successful managers realize the importance of feedback and use it appropriately. Your quality management system needs a lot of individual feedback moving through the organization.

Giving individual feedback is an expression of caring, especially if it involves a performance failure and is thus a difficult task for the manager. Why caring? Well, it is a good news–bad news situation: The bad news is that the employee learns that all is not well and some improvement is necessary. The good news is that the person can do something about it. That is a lot more caring than quietly "documenting" someone's failures and then firing the person. It is caring because the manager also takes on the additional job of noticing the improved behavior and responding to it.

Is there an analog in the case of organizational feedback? The answer, of course, is yes. But the mechanics are a bit more complex than simply observing and tracking individual performance. For a quality management system, getting closure on system operation, evaluating the operation of the system against baselines, making adjustments, and doing it all over again keep the system tuned up and ensure continuous improvement.

The Elements of Continuous Improvement

Feedback plays a three-part role in the quest for continuous improvement. Managers use feedback for three reasons:

1. To control the operation
2. To track and respond to unit performance that meets, exceeds, or fails to meet expectations
3. To provide a sound basis for recognition and perhaps even celebration

Controlling the Operation

If they are to control its performance, managers must know how an organization is doing. If it is supposed to make a profit, they must know the status of its profitability. In every case, they need to be concerned about the use of resources, particularly how they perform against the capital and expense budget. *Control* is defined as a process using mechanisms and methods to ensure that managerial and organizational objectives are met by comparing actual performance to a standard. Through control, things happen the way they are supposed to happen; it is future-focused. In the area of quality, that could mean achieving world-class performance levels.

Some experts take potshots at the idea of control out of a concern that it flies in the face of prevention of defects in a "total quality" sense on the one hand and breakthrough approaches to quality improvements on the other. Neither criticism is accurate. Both relate more to a quality system than to a management system. There is nothing about managerial control that says that present levels of control are good enough. Control is not going away, but it has to be handled sensitively.

Information access is inherent in the control process. We all agree with that. But what makes the process a bit different in a quality management system is in the delegation of authority and the empowerment to make decisions, along with the accompanying risks.

Suppose you have accepted the responsibility for a six-month project; your boss has provided a reasonable budget to pull it off along with the broad, open-ended charter to do what you have to do to get the job done. Sounds great—power, freedom, flexibility, and potential reward! Who could ask for anything more? You start to work and two weeks later, the boss calls you into her office and probes in some detail about the status of your project. Specifically, she questions an expenditure for an inexpensive software tracking package. She expresses concern that it is not sufficiently comprehensive.

What do you do from then on? You very likely check with her on every small decision to avoid what you perceive as having your judgment questioned. What has happened to the delegation? How empowered do you feel?

The situation is clear: The two of you failed to agree on what information was needed to move upward, at what time, on what schedule, and in how much detail. This happens all the time. Expectations are not always clarified; people do not automatically appreciate one another's information needs or preferred ways of processing information (e.g., reading, listening). This leads to the evaporation of "delegation."

Now, put all this in the context of a red-hot priority job for a task force. The task force members have a charter to work on a mainstream, bottom-line change to a manufacturing process. There are "big bucks" riding on the outcome. The CEO himself has been involved, and so has his reputation. The task force has been working for three weeks, and the executive contact is breathing down the neck of any task force member in sight for status information, commitments to an expedited schedule, and the like. What has happened here? The same thing as with the individual project: There is work going on, and there is a management structure. Members of management are attempting on a good-faith basis to exercise control. They are responding to their sense of risk and their accountability to the organization and its leadership.

Control is an absolutely legitimate and essential management function. But how it is exercised is fundamental to the success of quality management initiatives. This is true for work units that take on a quality team role and their managers; it is especially true for any "ad-hocracies" such as quality task forces that have important work to do but no ongoing reputation, no close team or personal relationships to glue things together, and no established (and trusting) reporting relationship.

What are managers to do? One thing they should not do is abandon the control process. Actions that should happen are the following:

- Quality teams and task forces must identify critical information (usually an exception to a standard that is not a normal variation) that must move up the line. They have to know when and through which channels.
- Communication that is formatted in some way is fundamental to managing new or expanded information flows. It makes sense to use pages from TQMetrics to flow upward to the next-level Master Manual, at which point Master Manual pages can continue to flow upward level by level.
- There has to be some sort of acknowledgment of and reaction to the various items moving through the organization. To have something drop through a crack will destroy the system's credibility. The feedback requires feedback, i.e., reinforcement.

Tracking Performance

The whole idea of continuous improvement and deployment of learning through success stories dictates having organizational mechanisms for tapping and tracking information, followed by an organizational response. This is the familiar cycle of setting objectives or goals, providing resources, tracking performance, giving feedback, rewarding success (or recycling a disappointment), and going on to the next level.

Survey-Feedback Process

Organizations have tapped and tracked quality management information in as many ways as the mind can imagine. The best way is the one that works and fits the organization's culture. Early in the book, we suggested the use of a survey process. Surveys based on useful models are excellent tools for acquiring status information, tracking progress, and even soliciting creative ideas through written comments. Surveys allow benchmarking and comparisons within an organization and with other organizations. They have the advantages of easy assessment of results and easy storage and transfer of data.

The Baldrige Award is an overall model that can be replicated in survey format. The 1,000 points involved in scoring can be converted to 100 items and readily measured. It would be easiest to use 200 items and a five-point scale (200 X 5 = 1000), but that number of items is cumbersome. It takes longer to take the survey, and capturing its essence requires sophisticated analysis to understand what the issues are. For example, a factor analysis process will identify clusters of items that hang together statistically to give an efficient and economic interpretation of results. That can run into a lot more than a few dollars for processing and interpretation. One hundred items with the same five-point scale can be multiplied by two to approximate the Baldrige Award scoring process.

With a small group, a survey can be hand-tallied and averaged; the top ten and bottom ten items can be identified and fed back to the quality team or task force for discussion and response. This can be repeated on the next set of twenty items and/or on a chronological or as-needed basis over indefinite periods of time.

The key to the successful use of surveys is to use them constructively: no witchhunts. Senior people should not push to see scores from lower levels; it is more appropriate and functional to provide them with lists of top and bottom items without scores. It would be nice to argue for voluntary exchange of survey information, but that simply will not work in a major system change in which coordination is needed across boundaries and levels and resources have to be allocated to bolster areas and initiatives that are lagging.

Team Process Outputs

Output from the team process and the TQMeetings process can also be used to tap and track information. But both these activities need to be nurtured. As noted earlier, there is nothing inherent in a team process that will keep enthusiasm up and the process running indefinitely. Someone in the organization has to pass on success stories and articles from publications. Someone has to monitor the videotape market for new tools. Someone has to come up with new ideas for topics to be discussed. Someone has to obtain needed resources such as equipment for team sessions—e.g., overhead projector, flip charts, fresh markers. Someone has to recognize when coordination between teams will avoid negative ripples or prevent overlapping and unproductive efforts. If the quality management system is being implemented at a low level by one manager, all these things fall into his or her lap and must be handled if the change process is to work.

Suggestion Systems

Suggestion systems have been around for a long time. There has always been a philosophical argument that they are redundant, since part of every employee's or associate's job is to suggest improvements. The countervailing argument is that you will get more and better suggestions if there is a fair and responsive reward system. In most settings, the multiple overlapping task forces and quality teams involved in the introduction of a quality management system render the suggestion system obsolete. The benefits that are generated by successful suggestions should be spread around the new entities.

There are historical challenges facing suggestion systems that have to be recognized and managed: Deciding who gets what and when covers most of the tough calls. It is always difficult to determine fair and equitable participation in rewards, and determining when to reward can be a problem with complicated suggestions. Should the reward be given right away, or when the suggestion begins to pay off? Senior managers may shy away from giving organizational recognition out of fear that they may go too far or too fast in giving credit or not far or fast enough. How are quality suggestions to be evaluated if the results are not readily quantifiable? Should everyone who produces a creative new idea be recognized in some way? Should rewards consist of letters and certificates only? Should all awards be tied to quality progress with some kind of logo or symbol?

The total quality movement has spawned numerous task forces to hammer out solutions to these challenging problems. For those without experience with suggestion systems but who are interested in using one within the context of implementing a quality management system, there is the National Association of Suggestion Systems (NASS) and extensive industry experience. NASS reminds anyone setting up a suggestion system to have a designated contact point, be able to describe how the system works, be able to make decisions promptly, and have a scale of rewards; cash, along with trips, may be most popular, but savings bonds and noncash awards such as certificates for a night on the town or tickets to an event are also popular and easy to administer. An effective way to provide broad participation while limiting financial exposure is to have drawings in which people participate as a result of their contributions, the number of opportunities that are sometimes weighted in terms of quantity or value. Good documentation is critical to the proper allocation of rewards and the prevention of duplication. Safety programs and formal productivity programs are excellent analogs for organization-wide recognition initiatives. There is a clear overlap between productivity improvements sought through mechanisms such as the Scanlon plan and quality assurance progress. There is a close connection between historical efforts, such as Scanlon, and today's gain-sharing compensation plans.

Organizational Audits

Another performance-tracking technique that has an excellent pay-off is the organizational audit. Units can audit themselves by means of a task force, or they can be audited by headquarters. Sophisticated companies have been doing this for years. Exxon USA's human resources department brought in an outside expert to assess its performance through the eyes of its internal customers; it used an inside team for the same purpose on a more complex basis. The company also simulated inspections by the Office of Federal Contract Compliance (OFCC) to ensure that its field location processes were appropriate and functioning properly. Federal Express brought in a team to do multiple audits of its readiness for a Baldrige Award site visit the year it won the Award. The Baldrige site visit is essentially an audit, as are the ISO 9000 precertification and certification visits.

An organization can audit its performance against its overall Master Manual as well as by level and division. Identified variations and gaps can be addressed, and the process can be recycled at some future point to generate feedback.

Giving Recognition

Recognition is an important component of the successful implementation of new systems. What is rewarded tends to be repeated. Punishment is not the answer to nonperformance. The essence of punishment is to stop undesired behavior. The criminal justice analog is to throw someone in jail, or worse. Punishment leaves a vacuum until another process is identified and guides the introduction and maintenance of desired behavior.

A quality management system is a blessing when an organization is working out a way to reward valuable contributions. Why? Specific objectives and goals are already set out in the Master Manual, and the mechanisms are in place to track data to support accomplishments. There are also the advantages of the benchmarking philosophy, practice, and resources. It is a lot easier to compensate an organization that is among the best or, better still, world-class and performing well financially. The American Productivity and Quality Center's benchmarking initiative that was launched in 1992 will go a long way toward simplifying the benchmarking process and adding to its validity. Its new Benchmarking Award will stimulate and reward participation in the process.

Relatively few organizations have team-based compensation, but it is an area of growing interest. For the moment, individual financial incentives are still in a merit-pay format; executive bonuses are still where the big bucks are. Coming along, though, are creative efforts to recognize contributions to financial performance at lower levels and to compensate team accomplishments. Initially, the steps involved are to modify performance appraisal systems so that related individual behaviors (e.g., team player, creative contributor) are factored into an overall individual appraisal through additional or modified scales.

Companies should keep everything they do in the management system area as simple and easily understandable as possible. As a goal "going for the gold" in the sense of massive management improvements, if needed, is appropriate over a reasonable period of time. But a whirlwind of new and complex initiatives does not make any sense, even if the organization needs a whole lot of work. There is always a clear and present danger of things collapsing of their own weight. Experience says that companies with little sophistication and a lot of need to improve should start very simply. Capable and strong organizations can rev up rapidly.

The key management skills are pacing new initiatives, balancing interests and obligations, and anticipating organizational ripples that may damage credibility and frustrate progress.

11

Continuous Improvement: Evergreen in Action

You should now be ready to open your campaign for quality *management*. Here are a few thoughts to bolster your motivation to act. On a national basis, we are in deep trouble if we think provincially, rely on protectionism, live in the past, move slowly, educate and develop too poorly, and fail to give top priority to quality and productivity. At the level of the individual enterprise, we are in deep competitive trouble without total employee and associate involvement in organizational improvement, continuous attention to improvement, and a strong customer orientation both internally and externally. But if the total management quality culture is created and endures, the enterprise can look forward to enhanced profitability and longevity.

Managers are focusing their quality efforts in the wrong place. They have been pushed to micromanage *quality* management; it would be far better to apply their energies to creating a quality *management* system. Of the three major tools—the Trilogy, the Triad, and the Evergreen System—the Evergreen System is so important that this final chapter is devoted to it alone.

There are two important steps to take before looking at the Evergreen System. The first involves *formalizing a set of quality management values*. Every manager should have some idea of what is important in terms of how organizations are managed. There are four areas to concentrate on.

1. *Mobilize organizational energies toward specific purposes.* Facilitate upward influence and contributions through open communication (don't shoot the messenger, and don't micromanage) and ongoing

expressions of interest and emphasis. Keep actions focused by communicating expectations and boundaries, highlighting areas for examination, and asking for assistance in dealing with specific situations.

2. *Use time and resources effectively.* You need feedback to know what is going on, and you must be able to decide what to influence to improve performance. You need to be able to tailor your actions to the situation and appropriately affect policies, procedures, objectives, standards, budgets, programs, and performance systems. You can examine and alter key processes and achieve leverage through delegation and empowerment.

3. *Compare effectiveness periodically; apply benchmarking concepts if possible.* Comparisons can be made among your personal standards and expectations, a model of organizational effectiveness such as your own Master Manual (or a component such as the Baldrige Award), a database (such as the American Productivity and Quality Center's International Benchmarking Clearinghouse), history, or partner organizations. Clarify what is revealed in the comparison process by widespread involvement and action planning for progress. Continue to recycle.

4. *Keep the system alive and the organization turned on.* Once installed, systems *must* be given attention. The natural state of systems is to move from a state of growth through a state of vitality to a state of decay. The concept of the plant analogy of a little sunshine and a little water is absolutely appropriate for organizational systems. You must have feedback to know what is going on; you must take the organization's temperature. Benchmarking serves an important purpose by keeping attention focused on key areas. Personal leadership generates the energy to keep the organization vital; cheerleading, visibility, involvement, and vitality help enormously. It is essential to do something special periodically. You want to do things that are sensible, relevant, and practical, but beyond that, there is a wide range of initiatives that will keep an organization and its people turned on: special events, contests, surveys, state-of-the-system meetings, videotape programs, barbecues. The key is not so much what you do, but finding the time to do it.

The second step is to ensure that *the criteria for making decisions and setting priorities are the organization's mission, objectives, and strategic and operating plans.* This statement borders on being self-evident, but things are sometimes forgotten or overlooked in the heat of battle, even though they may have been handled carefully at some earlier point in the business calendar. Thus this reminder: The best managers keep their eyes on what makes a difference.

The Evergreen Approach

Managers who have been involved with organizational improvement activities over the years have learned a lot about installing systems. The biggest challenge always seems to be getting a new system to last over the long haul. The needed process and structures constitute the Evergreen approach that was first explored in Chapter 2.

The Evergreen approach in matrix form has twenty-eight elements—fourteen for process and fourteen for structure (see Exhibit 11-1). As you know, these elements must be considered and acted upon during initial planning if the system is to last. Getting the system to last is the area where most mistakes are made in designing and installing new systems: Some Evergreen elements do get attention before the launch, but others are handled only when they become problems, or not at all. What has to be in place for a system to *last* must be put in place (or scheduled) *first*.

To make Evergreen even more relevant at this point, Exhibit 11-1 depicts the matrix in terms of a critique of the Baldrige Award model. Did the Baldrige system designers touch all the Evergreen bases? The answer is a respectful no. They did a tremendous job, but there is room for improvement. The Award attends to executive leadership, but it does not focus on the stability of that leadership in terms of the people involved. Yet the companies that have been successful have had that stability and an accompanying constancy of purpose.

The matrix lists the actions that are necessary *and* sufficient for installing a long-lasting system involving a major change. Note the top-to-bottom distinction between process and structure. It is generally helpful to categorize actions in this way to better communicate their expected contributions. Next, note the left-to-right evaluation of the Guidelines in terms of their actual contribution to the actions needed for a long-haul quality management installation. There are both pluses and minuses.

The current Baldrige Award Guidelines can and should be supplemented. The investment in launching a quality or other major system demands the most effective possible approach to managing change.

If you were to use the matrix as a checklist, how many dimensions could you check as being in good shape? Do you end up with the potential for two columns—one strong and one weak or missing? Is there a pattern that shows that you are in better shape for structure than for process? Is there a message there? What steps should you take to optimize your Evergreen situation?

Exhibit 11-1. The Evergreen matrix.

Baldrige Weaknesses	*Baldrige Strengths*

Process

- Prepared for STRETCH goals, objectives.
- Consistent with owner financial interests.
- Fits well with economic climate, environment.
- Realistic bases to attract commitment and innovation.
- Provides clear "pluses" for the organization, sound bases for a culture shift.
- Fits organizational rhythms and calendar.
- Initial activities loaded for success.

- Congruence with mission, charter.
- Leadership understands, buys into all implications.
- Tested against anticipated future developments.
- Provides involvement, empowerment for key players.
- Provides psychological value to those impacted.
- Contains recognition, reward opportunities for all.
- Realistic time demands, schedules established.

Structure

- Executive leadership stable, committed.
- Progress/process reviews defined as to content, schedule, follow-up.
- Stewardship results, methods established.
- Measurement and evaluation processes known.
- Standard operating procedures (SOPs) are in place, tested.
- Protocols set to solve problems, manage interfaces, and deal with scarcity.
- Needed resources are at hand or accessible.

- Champions identified; TQ process defined.
- Organizational commitments are "public."
- Planning system is in place; key dates are set.
- Budget process is activated, controls established.
- Task forces/teams are designated, prepared, trained.
- Linkages between internal, external suppliers and customers established, ripples anticipated.
- Communication system, programs are operational.

The Wrap-Up

There is a powerful potential in the TQM Trilogy and its supporting TQ Triad and Evergreen approach for all managers and many staff professionals, especially those who aspire to move into the ranks of management. The potential involves optimizing the management of individual organizations and their profitability. But just as important, perhaps more, is the potential to enhance the nation's competitiveness and economic performance. This book is your tool kit for action.

Appendixes

Appendix A
A Worldwide Quality Perspective

Quality, as we now think of it, is a blending of several proud traditions. The nineteenth-century American crafts culture went underground during the scientific management revolution, but threads of both contributed to the extraordinary production accomplishments of World War II.

Low levels of postwar competition led to a weakening of the quality imperative until it was recently reawakened in many key industries by the success of competition from Japan and other Asian countries. The "new" quality has emerged as a much broader concept than before—integrating technical issues with behavioral concepts and progressive managerial practices to give quality a form that veteran practitioners have trouble recognizing.

Quality can be defined in a number of ways. Older definitions emphasize fidelity to a set of final product or service standards or specifications worked out by the organization with perhaps some reference to customers' interests. More recent definitions feature customers' complete satisfaction, even delight, with the final product or service. The most recent definitions also recognize that the organization itself needs to design, install, and operate high-quality internal processes that allow customer satisfaction to occur. The organization must operate in a strategic context that is satisfactory to all stakeholders, not just customers.

Relationship to Productivity

Productivity starts from a definition that relates an amount of physical output to its related labor input. More recent work has recognized that other inputs (e.g., capital, materials, energy, business services) are appropriately the subject of productivity analysis and that output, especially in support groups or service providers, may not be clearly physical. Output should not be counted unless it is "good" output. Thus we find quite a convergence between organizational productivity improvement and organizational process quality improvement. Both are aimed at customers' interest in better (and lower-cost) products and services and are achieved through balanced systems improvement.

TQM: A Comprehensive Management Improvement Philosophy

Total quality management (TQM) provides the best current example of a comprehensive management improvement philosophy. Even this comes in different flavors and sizes, but the "total" in total quality management has three fundamental aspects: horizontal, vertical, and strategic.

Horizontal means that the fundamental unit of analysis is the business process that cuts its way across the organization, starting with external suppliers, passing through operational and/or support groups of the organization, and ending with a final customer. Every person or subgroup making up part of the process has one or more immediate suppliers and one or more immediate customers, most of which are internal to the organization. Each supplier-customer interface should demonstrate the care and attention normally associated with external contacts. Departmental membership is an organizational convenience but should not influence the effort put into a process.

Vertical means that all levels of the organization have adopted the basic quality ethic and apply it in the processes they influence. Quality is not the exclusive interest of production workers, or of executives, or of first-line supervisors. Problem-solving teams often have members from several organizational levels.

Finally, the subject of the improvement effort must be that which is strategically important to the organization. Improvement efforts can start out with pilots or "practice" initiatives, but ultimately there must be a linkage between the main subject matter of the various improvement teams and the priority needs of the organization as identified in strategic planning exercises. That is where the quality circles of the late 1970s and early 1980s fell short of the original expectation. They were generally established within single departments, choosing their improvement issues from the immediate neighborhood rather than focusing on issues that were of high priority to the entire organization.

What all TQM efforts have as underlying principles are continuous improvement, wall-to-wall involvement (every workstation a control point), and management by fact. The intent is that each worker at each level take it upon himself or herself to do the work right the first time, never pass on bad work, and strive to make improvements based on data received (or self-generated) concerning his or her processes.

The New Partnership: Integrating Behavioral Managerial Practices

A major feature of organizational improvement efforts is the attempt to flatten the organization and make it more flexible, usually through the use of teams. The classic organizational chart shows a steep hierarchy with as many as fifteen or twenty layers in the largest of plants. The new model favored by Japanese export-oriented industries is three or four levels in the typical plant: a plant manager, a production superintendent, possibly a product-line and/or area manager, and the standard team member. The team member is typically cross-trained to do several if not all of the tasks required of the team.

This sort of flat organization functions well only if managers have learned to communicate directly to standard workers without the need for filtering or interpretation and if workers have taken on at least some extra responsibility for ensuring that assigned work gets done well. This form of organization sounds very cost-effective; after all, several managerial layers have been removed. But much more planning and training are required to start up and nurture such an organization. It can usually succeed if it manages to serve the customer better through either faster response time or a more reliable product or service.

Not all teams created as part of productivity and quality initiatives are created to accomplish routine work in a leaner organization. There are also special, temporary quality teams created to solve a specific problem that has typically been identified in an assessment project. Unlike the situation in the quality circles discussed above, the nonvolunteer members of these teams are usually from different parts of the organization and have been identified because they make up part of the process being analyzed.

There are many types of teams, and an alert organization will be operating several different types for different purposes. It is critical that everyone understand what the teams are doing and how they fit together. Thus, regardless of structure, information sharing becomes a critical part of any quality initiative. This is the opposite of the "need-to-know" approach that is commonly practiced; the new presumption is that everyone needs access to nearly everything, with a few specific exceptions.

Always With Us: Technical Issues

Manufacturers, following Japanese experience in some industries, are recognizing the shortcomings of economies of scale as a manufacturing theme. As customer satisfaction becomes the main strategic driver, customers are learning to demand shorter lead times for existing supplied products and services and to feel free to change specifications on short notice. Once one company in an industry is able and willing to cater to the customers' changing tastes, all companies in the industry have to at least consider offering the same level of flexibility.

From an equipment point of view, the desired feature is now flexibility and not necessarily size, speed, or power. The idea of quick changeover, which applies to service areas in addition to die-containing machinery, is now a major improvement goal. "Just in time" manufacturing, utilizing flexible machinery and equally flexible machine operators and support people, has brought revolutionary change to many companies.

A major effect of flexibility is a severe reduction in the work-in-process inventory caused by scheduling. Once a unit is started, it tends to flow on through and be finished and shipped. Extensive quality training of the line workers usually accompanies this shift in philosophy, so work in process that is accumulated due to quality defects is also reduced.

Advances are also being made in design. Concurrent engineering recognizes that much of the complex design-manufacture-market cycle can be overlapped and thus reduced in order to hit the market earlier in response to competition. It is now becoming commonplace to train "ordinary" workers—blue- and white-collar—to participate in systems redesign work, using flowcharts of the process in which these people work.

Measurement and Feedback

Flatter organizations, more flexible scheduling, and progressive management practices all call for more attention to the performance measurement and feedback cycle. It is now recognized that all employees need measures of their performance and the performance of their processes in order to stimulate grass-roots improvement. Measurement of improvement trends must be done everywhere in the organization, not just at the finished product stage seen by the outside world. Rarely is a single measure sufficient at any level of the organization. There is always a dynamic interplay among productivity, quality, cycle time, utilization, on-time delivery, safety, creativity, and many other aspects of work. Thus a "family" of measures is called for, typically resulting in a performance index for each work group within an organization.

Improvement is the major goal, but continuous improvement, with its gradualist implication, is not sufficient in many competitive realities. A new emphasis is being placed on benchmarking. This includes identifying where the best examples of implementation of a particular process can be found and consequent goal setting aimed at equaling or exceeding that best practice in a planned time frame.

Appendix B

A Training Curriculum Model

The following ten potential training areas are intended to be used to tentatively identify training needs for various kinds of employees or associates. No one person or group needs all the training listed. Differences among organization levels must be considered.

Potential Total Management Quality Course Descriptions

1. *Quality economics.* Investigation of current economic challenges; broad spectrum of economic development as a national imperative; international considerations of relative power (e.g., knowledge, wealth, and force); the implications of economic close-coupling; implications of the labor component in a firm's activities; ways in which a total quality system positively affects an organization's bottom line.

2. *Total Quality Management (TQM) systems.* Philosophy and concepts of TQM systems; performance improvement potential; history of major contributors (Deming, Juran, Crosby, Grayson); basic TQM vocabulary and definitions; relation to earlier movements; ISO 9000/Deming Prize/Baldrige Award implications; state-level and professional accreditation replications of the Baldrige process; typical TQM models and approaches; supplier-operation-customer model; labor unions and TQM; experiences of Baldrige Award participants (GAO's *Management Practices* Study); employee involvement, empowerment to act; task force arrangements; documentation (e.g., Master Manual).

3. *Performance management.* Systems approach to organizational design; value system impact; measuring and dealing with organizational culture(s); obtaining commitment; creativity and innovation; behavior modification and reward strategies; role of leadership at all levels; task

force and quality team operations; group decision-making techniques; work design principles; internal consultation roles and skills; organizational diagnosis methods; inter- and intragroup communications.

4. *Quality metrics.* Design of research studies and statistical control methods; problem-solving and decision-making process review; historical analysis and future forecasting methods; Pareto analysis, flow diagrams, cause-and-effect diagrams, fishbones, scatter diagrams, control charts, regression and multivariate analyses; special techniques for identifying customer needs and expectations; questionnaire and instrument design; focus group and observation approaches; quality testing concepts and procedures; overview of descriptive, inferential, and predictive statistics.

5. *Quality management.* Creation of learning designs and delivery methods; training needs analysis (targets, time allocations); internal consulting skills; cost-benefit analyses; validation and evaluation of results; keys to effective transfer of training to the job; methods of instruction (classroom, on-the-job training, coaching); remote delivery approaches; training logistics; training documentation; audiovisual hardware and software; computers and other electronic devices; evaluating external training sources.

6. *Information systems.* Organizational applications of information, data, and systems analysis; review of problem-solving and decision-making processes; utilization of computer hardware, software, and languages; investments in equipment, custom programming; off-the-rack software availability and use; communication systems and networking; record storage and retrieval; security systems; support of quality management processes that include benchmarking and data exchanges with electronic documentation and data analysis.

7. *Law, ethics, and management.* Legal exposure and consequences; approaches to co-ventures and limited partnerships; establishing special supplier relationships; protecting patents, copyrights, and trademarks; special attention to intellectual property ownership; publications and public appearances; obligation of Baldrige Award winners to share expertise and experiences; proprietary and privileged information; information release; guarantees and warranties; applications of mediation and arbitration; contracts with labor unions; wage-hour laws (time for quality activities); ethical issues relevant for the local organization.

8. *Negotiating agreements.* Organizational objectives in bargaining activities; representative models and protocols; supplier and customer interactions; handling disputes; effective techniques for external interactions; achieving customer acceptance; horizontal bargaining and negotiation on an intraorganizational basis; unions and collective bargain-

ing agreements; cooperation versus conflict; conflict-reduction skills; individual interfacing skills; upward negotiations for approvals and resources within an organization; development of related presentation skills.

9. *Human resources management.* Human resources contributions to QMS activation and maintenance; implications of work force education and diversity; labor-management cooperation; employee/associate communications methods and procedures; individual and group awards and recognition; merit systems and performance-based compensation, including group compensation/gain-sharing plans; payments for suggestions, contest approaches; wage-hour laws and team activities; employee safety and health.

10. *Managing transformations.* Applying effective change-management technologies; basic model: inform, involve, educate, reinforce, confront; using pilot programs; transformational leadership; gaining employee acceptance; measuring progress toward new cultural dimensions; extended time lines and sustained interest; self-managing teams (removal of work group supervision); potential changes to performance appraisal systems; influencing individual motivation and reward; consensus goal setting; using conflict management protocols; union involvement and changes in collective bargaining agreements; operational start-ups; Evergreen strategies for change management.

Appendix C
Limited and Emerging Awards

The five quality initiatives presented and discussed in this appendix are equated in Exhibit C-1.

NASA Award

The oldest major quality award is the National Aeronautics and Space Administration (NASA) Quality and Excellence Award, which was created in 1985 to stimulate attention to quality by NASA's contractors, which make up about 85 percent of the work force at NASA installations. The Award was recently renamed to honor George M. Low, a former deputy administrator of NASA. There is balanced attention to process and performance, with ample mention of customer satisfaction, human resources initiatives, and top-management issues in addition to quality assurance techniques.

There are large- and small-business categories. The typical pattern has been two winners—usually both large businesses, although a small business won in 1990. The finalists are announced publicly, and it is typical for those that do not win in one year to keep reapplying until they do. The site visits and later debriefings are of significant help to the applicants, and there is a good record of continued long-term improvement by winners. The evaluation criteria (1,000-point maximum score) are as follows:

Points

1.0   *Performance achievements (600 points total)*
1.1   Customer satisfaction

Exhibit C-1.   Comparison of five quality initiatives.

	ISO 9000	*Deming*	*Baldrige*	*NASA*	*Shingo*
Year Created	1987	1951	1987	1985	1988
Basic Form	Certification	Long-Term Prize	Annual Contest	Annual Contest	Annual Contest
Winners	Many	Few	Few	Few	Few
Emphasis	Organization Policy Documentation	Statistics; Problem Solving	Customer Leadership; Support Organization; Measurement; Benchmarking	Customer Leadership; Employee Involvement	Flexible Manufacturing Improvements Customer Results; Employee Empowerment
Absent	Customer Results	Customer Objectives	——	——	Documentation Detail
Cost	Low–Medium	High	Medium—High	Low–Medium	Low

Points

1.1.1	Contract performance 120
1.1.2	Schedule 50
1.1.3	Cost 50
1.2	Quality
1.2.1	Quality assurance (QA) 120
1.2.2	Vendor QA, involvement 50
1.2.3	External communication 40
1.2.4	Problem prevention, resolution 40
1.3	Productivity
1.3.1	Software utilization 40
1.3.2	Process improvement, equipment modernization 30
1.3.3	Resources conservation 30
1.3.4	Effective use of human resources 30

Points

2.0	*Process achievements (400 points total)*	
2.1	Commitment and communication	
2.1.1	Top management commitment/involvement	100
2.1.2	Goals, planning, and measurement	80
2.1.3	Internal communication	40
2.2	Human resources activities	
2.2.1	Training	50
2.2.2	Work force involvement	50
2.2.3	Awards and recognition	40
2.2.4	Health and safety	40

Shingo Prize

A relatively new award growing in impact is the Shingo Prize for Excellence in American Manufacturing. Its purpose is to promote world-class manufacturing and to recognize companies that excel in productivity and process improvement, quality enhancement, and customer satisfaction. It was established by Dr. Shigeo Shingo, a Japanese author, consultant, and one of the leading experts on improving the manufacturing process. He trained more than 10,000 people in over 100 companies. Until his recent death, he served as the president of Japan's Institute of Management Improvement. He was instrumental in the development of many flexible manufacturing and just-in-time techniques that now make up the Toyota Production System.

The Shingo Prize is sponsored and managed by the Utah State University Partner's Program and is open to manufacturers of any size. There is no limit as to number of winners; since start-up in 1989, there has been one small-business recipient in each year in 1989, 1990, and 1991; three large-business recipients in 1991; and two large-business recipients in 1992. There is also a research and professional publication prize that is awarded at three levels.

The Shingo criteria emphasize manufacturing improvements. Anecdotal evidence is welcomed but must be accompanied by measured improvement in productivity, quality, and customer satisfaction. The criteria also mention leadership, employee involvement, support systems integration, and other broader issues, but there is tolerance of a wide variety of alternative approaches. The 1993–1994 Shingo criteria are as follows:

Points

1. *Total quality and productivity management culture and infrastructure (275 points total)*

    A. Leading   100
    B. Empowering   100
    C. Partnering (with relevant stakeholders)   75

2. *Manufacturing strategy, processes, and systems (425 points total)*

    A. Manufacturing vision and strategy   50
    B. Manufacturing process integration   125
    C. Quality and productivity methods integration   125
    D. Manufacturing and business integration   125

3. *Measured quality and productivity (200 points total)*

    A. Productivity improvement   100
    B. Quality enhancement   100

4. *Customer satisfaction (100 points total)*

5. *Summary of achievements (unscored, two-page quick reference document)*

Exhibit C-1 compares five quality initiatives: the Shingo and the NASA, and the three making up the TQM Trilogy: the Baldrige, Deming, and ISO 9000.

Federal Awards

There are important programs in the U.S. federal government to award special performance in specific agencies, but these have not reached the awareness level and stature of the Baldrige Award, which is much more broadly known.

State-Level Awards

A few states have taken advantage of federal legislation to create Senate Productivity Awards. Under the auspices of one or both U.S. senators, states such as Virginia, Alabama, and Maryland give annual awards to companies in several categories. These awards are usually presented at well-attended and publicized conferences. The awards are normally administered by a productivity or quality center in the state.

Some other states such as North Carolina, Connecticut, and Minnesota have created local versions of the Baldrige Award, using identical or similar criteria and administration methods. The Texas Quality Award, created in 1992, has added categories for not-for-profit (e.g., health care) and educational institutions in addition to large and small businesses.

Foreign Awards

Awards are beginning to appear in foreign countries (other than Japan). Mexico has an award modeled after the Baldrige Award but has added criteria for environmental effects (such as ecosystem preservation), development of small suppliers, and community action. There are also awards in Canada, Australia, and some European countries in addition to an all-Europe award: The European Quality Award (TEQA).

TEQA is administered by the European Foundation for Quality Management, which is located in the Netherlands. It is for organizations based in Western Europe (although the "Western" concept may have limited future viability). To receive an award, a company must demonstrate that its approach to total quality management has contributed significantly over the past few years to satisfying the expectations of customers, employees, and others with an interest in the company. It is clearly a broad-gauge management tool; conceptually it is close to the Baldrige Award, but point values differ. The first awards were presented in late 1992. The award criteria (adding up to 100 percent) are as follows:

Percentage

Customer satisfaction	20
People (management, feelings)	18
Business results (achievement relative to plan)	15
Processes (management of value-added activities)	14
Leadership (toward TQM transformation)	10
Resources (management, utilization, and preservation of financial, informational, technological)	9
Policy and strategy (vision, values, and direction)	8
Impact on society	6

* * *

Awards of this sort can have value to an organization in many ways. Most commentators focus on the direct effects. Winners get important publicity for their products and services. Sometimes this can even lead to new contacts or contracts. There is certainly at least a temporary effect on morale in the winning organization. Even nonwinners can talk of direct effects. The team that prepared the application learned a great deal about the organization and perhaps something about teamwork and cooperation under pressure. The feedback from the examiners is of value to the organization whether it wins or loses.

There are also some valuable indirect effects. The assessing organization that acts on its findings develops a cadre of change agents who can literally transform the organization, given enough time and support. An organization that submits to the discipline of an assessment gradually becomes a drivable organization, where accountability and responsibility—even in the lower ranks—become standard practice. The organization becomes accustomed to acting on new facts once a challenge is put into focus. It is in this indirect sense that the true value of the awards comes out. An award, whether external or simply internal to the organization, helps create a focus on key issues and the confidence to attack those issues with an expectation of success. The trick is to select the right focus for each specific organization.

Other indirect values include building a common vocabulary among all the diverse elements of an organization and being able to build pride into contributions. Jobs actually become fun when there is a new or renewed commitment to excellence in daily work.

Appendix D

A Grass-Roots System Outline

Following is a grass-roots installation model:

1. Decision to investigate/implement new management approaches by CEO
2. Decision meetings with senior executives, using decision tools such as a ranking instrument, questionnaire, worksheet:
   - Inform; explore issues.
   - Clarify purpose and objectives.
   - Explore three levels: (a) organization and its interfaces, (b) essential organizational transformational processes, and (c) roles at managerial and individual levels.
   - Obtain agreement on actions, sequence, time line(s).
   - Get commitment; identify natural leaders.
3. Definition of "breakthrough" organizational vision (world-class, tough, major achievements, if needed; otherwise, essential incremental achievements)
4. Specification of mission(s): executive committee (cabinet); significant organizational elements
   - Consider modern leadership, theories of organizational culture.
   - Compare/contrast with existing organization.
   - Define an ideal (leadership, processes, structure).
   - Plan steps to achieve ideal.
5. Analysis and benchmarking of the organization's present quality orientation/processes (TQM inventory/survey)
   - Uncover plans, goals, processes that are incomplete with respect to quality needs, interests.
   - Analyze present situation against the standard TQM supplier-process-customer-quality model; identify deficiencies.

- Establish evidence of previous successes without quality emphasis.
6. Identification of customers (by segment, niche)
7. Identification of customer needs, expectations
8. Definition of essential quality processes for attention
9. Identification and definition of related metrics, controls (which to keep, change)
   - Rationale; importance of self-measurement, self-study
   - Retrieval of data
   - Analysis and assessment
   - Utilization
10. Establishment of supplier considerations
    - Communication
    - Favored status
    - Audit arrangements (tie-in to ISO 9000 process)
    - Support, other linkages (e.g., training)
11. Establishment of strategic plan with quality focus (three to ten years out, depending on organization)
12. Development of annual plan:
    - Start-up/breakthrough/Evergreen
    - Replication of above steps
13. Revision of roles, responsibilities, accountabilities
14. Development of new or revised human resources processes (as necessary)
    - Communication
    - Recognition
    - Reward (compensation, incentive bonuses)
    - Performance appraisal
    - Labor union(s) interface, bargaining
    - Training and development
    - Cultural transformation
15. Strategic and annual planning at significant lower levels
16. Design of launch and operating system(s)
17. Formation of steering committees/task forces
    - Cross-functional
    - Various levels, interlocked
    - "Pilot" approach at outset
    - Mission: gaining and maintaining continuous progress
18. Training (multiple audiences; multiple topics)
19. Ongoing activities
    - Task force meetings
    - Team meetings
    - Communication/coordination
    - Recognition
20. Review/resurvey processes; planning adjustments
21. Follow-up, recycling

Annotated Bibliography

Barry, Thomas J. *Quality Circles: Proceed with Caution.* Milwaukee: American Society for Quality Control, 1988.

The author examines quality circles through his twenty-eight years of management experience with IBM. He tells how to increase the effectiveness of participative management, sets down stringent guidelines for quality circle success, and describes the pitfalls if those guidelines aren't followed.

Berry, Thomas H. *Managing the Total Quality Transformation.* New York: McGraw-Hill, 1991.

Easy-to-follow action plan to reverse the downward spiral of poor quality. Arms readers with a complete operational strategy for designing, implementing, and sustaining a comprehensive quality process. Integrates the essential elements of various total quality management philosophies.

Brown, Mark Graham. *Baldrige Award Winning Quality.* White Plains, N.Y.: Quality Resources, 1991.

The author, a Baldrige Award examiner, covers the Award process and provides instructions for application by examination category and item; there is also a plan for conducting an audit process in preparation for a site visit.

Camp, Robert C. *Benchmarking: The Search for Industry Best Practices That Lead to Superior Performance.* Milwaukee: American Society for Quality Control, 1989.

This book explains the benchmarking process, including how to conduct investigations to ensure that an organization is based on industry-best practices. (Note: The American Productivity and Quality Center [123 N. Post Oak Lane, Houston, Texas, 77024, 713-681-4020] has a major benchmarking initiative under way with over eighty participating companies.)

Caroselli, Marlene. *Total Quality Transformations*. Amherst, Mass.: Human Resource Development Press, Inc., 1991.

This is a series of twelve interviews with quality leaders; it is practical in tone and supplies illustrations, summaries, and questions that would be helpful in designing workshops.

Christopher, William, and Carl G. Thor. *Handbook of Productivity Measurement and Improvement*. Cambridge, Mass.: Productivity Press, 1993.

This is a comprehensive tool kit for those interested in all aspects of the measurement process in organizations.

Collins, Frank C., Jr. *Quality: The Ball in Your Court*. Milwaukee: American Society for Quality Control, 1987.

Collins lays out a clear course of action to improve quality. He takes the reader inside dozens of foreign and domestic companies and analyzes weaknesses as well as strengths. Finally, he specifies fifteen steps to establish a quality improvement process.

Crosby, Phillip B. *Let's Talk Quality: 96 Questions You Always Wanted to Ask*. Cincinnati: Association for Quality and Participation, 1989.

A look at the major issues in quality improvement and management, in question-and-answer format. Crosby focuses on what quality really means, how to get it, what quality standards should be, and how to measure quality.

Crosby, Phillip B. *Quality Is Free: The Art of Making Quality Free*. New York: American Library, 1979.

Crosby shows how doing things right the first time adds nothing to the cost of a product or service.

Crosby, Phillip B. *Quality Without Tears: The Art of Hassle-Free Management*. New York: McGraw-Hill, 1984.

Covers Crosby's fourteen-step plan for fighting the secret enemies of quality, developing a quality culture, and getting all employees committed to quality.

Deming, W. Edwards. *Out of the Crisis*. Cambridge, Mass.: MIT Press, 1986.

Deming's statement of what American managers have been doing wrong and what they must do to correct the problem. The book contains his fourteen points for quality management.

Feigenbaum, Armand V. *Total Quality Control*. New York: McGraw-Hill, 1983.

This book tells how to plan a quality program, set up an appropriate organizational structure for implementing it, and direct all departments and the entire work force toward success.

Garvin, David A. *Managing Quality: The Strategic and Competitive Edge.* New York: Free Press, 1988.

The author describes eight dimensions of quality: performance, features, reliability, conformance, durability, serviceability, aesthetics, and perceived quality. He covers the history of quality, the major theorists, and how to compete on the basis of quality.

Gitlow, Howard S., and Shelly J. Gitlow. *Deming Guide to Quality and Competitive Position.* Cincinnati: Association for Quality and Participation, 1987.

A how-to guide to improving quality and productivity by type of organization. The book presents Deming's fourteen points for management as well as labor's eleven corollary points that integrate the efforts of management and labor.

Grayson, C. Jackson, Jr., and Carla O'Dell. *American Business: A Two-Minute Warning.* Houston: American Productivity and Quality Center, 1988.

This book lists ten changes that managers must make in order to survive into the twenty-first century. The authors demonstrate how government, management, and labor can work together to revive productivity and bolster the quality of American products.

Guaspari, John. *The Customer Connection: Quality for the Rest of Us.* New York: AMACOM, 1987.

This book tells you how to achieve improved quality for your organization. With humor, the author explores why quality got such a bad name in this country, why it is hard to meet quality objectives, and the customer-supplier relationship.

Guaspari, John. *I Know It When I See It: A Modern Fable About Quality.* New York: AMACOM, 1985.

This book is intended to guide managers to a new understanding of what quality really is and how to achieve it.

Harrington, H. James. *The Improvement Process: How America's Leading Companies Improve Quality.* Cincinnati: Association for Quality and Participation, 1987.

Based on a study of leading U.S. companies, this book shows what has been done to improve quality. It also explains how to start, evaluate, and improve a quality program in your organization.

Hart, Marilyn K., and Robert F. Hart. *Quantitative Methods for Quality and*

Productivity Improvement. Milwaukee: American Society for Quality Control, 1989.

This book explains the need for continuous improvement, presents the statistical methods for process control developed by Deming and Shewhart, and shows the limitations and alternatives of these methods.

Imai, Masaaki. *Kaizen: the Key to Japan's Competitive Success.* New York: Random House, 1986.

Kaizen means gradual, unending improvement and the setting and achieving of even higher standards. *Kaizen* is the secret behind Japan's economic "miracle." The author explores sixteen *kaizen* management practices with examples, case studies, charts, and graphs.

Ishikawa, Kaoru. *Guide to Quality Control.* Cincinnati: Association for Quality and Participation, 1986.

This book contains chapters on the basic statistical techniques used by quality circles and discusses several less familiar techniques. The author focuses on problem analysis and problem-solving techniques. Originally published by the Asian Productivity Organization (Tokyo, 1972).

Ishikawa, Kaoru. *What Is Total Quality Control? The Japanese Way.* Englewood Cliffs, N.J.: Prentice-Hall, 1985.

The author shows how to implement a total quality program based on customer satisfaction and describes how to build quality into the market research–production–sales cycle to attain defect-free products and services.

Jablowski, Joseph R. *Implementing Total Quality Management: An Overview.* San Diego: Pfeiffer & Co., 1991.

Significant behavioral science insights for program implementation; applies familiar and reliable "OD" approaches.

Juran, J. M. *Juran on Leadership for Quality: An Executive Handbook.* New York: Free Press, 1989.

Juran provides managers with specific methods they need to lead their companies on a quest for quality and discusses how to apply planning, control, and improvement to quality leadership.

Juran, J. M. *Juran on Planning for Quality.* New York: Free Press, 1988.

The author outlines the Juran Trilogy™: quality planning, quality control, and quality improvement. Topics include quality planning as a basic managerial process, as part of companywide quality management, and for departmental projects.

Juran, J. M., Frank M. Gryna, Jr., and R. S. Bingham, Jr., eds. *Quality Control Handbook.* 3d ed. New York: McGraw-Hill, 1974.

A theory and how-to guide to implementing a quality assurance system; a classic.

Kotter, John P., and James L. Heskett. *Corporate Culture and Performance.* New York: Free Press, 1992.

Going far beyond previous work, the authors provide the first comprehensive critical analysis of how the culture of an organization powerfully influences its economic performance. The authors describe how shared values and unwritten rules profoundly affect success or failure. They stress the need for continually responding to changing markets and new competitive environments and the importance of leadership in achieving success. Some of the companies studied have been involved in the Baldrige Award process.

Kume, Hitoshi, ed. *Statistical Methods for Quality Improvement.* Milwaukee: American Society for Quality Control, 1987.

This book contains articles written by quality control experts. It explores the tools of statistical methods and illustrates how the correct application of these tools improves the production process and reduces project defects. Exercises allow users to apply techniques to real-world problems.

Likert, Rensis. *The Human Organization: Its Management and Value.* New York: McGraw-Hill, 1967.

Describes a new and comprehensive system of management based on over twenty years of research at the University of Michigan. Likert describes a workable management system that can be used to achieve high productivity, above-average financial success, and improved labor relations. A systems approach has been substituted for piecemeal methods usually employed in efforts to improve an organization.

Mahoney, Francis X. *Creating Excellence: An Application of ISO 9000, the Deming Prize and Baldrige Award to Establish a Quality System.* New York: American Management Association, 1994.

A self-help executive extension course on improving organizational management, operating performance, quality, and productivity; describes how to make the best use of talent and experience already within the organization.

Mills, Charles A. *The Quality Audit: A Management Evaluation Tool.* Milwaukee: American Society for Quality Control, 1989.

This book examines the quality audit process from the viewpoints of the person requesting an audit, the organization being audited, and the auditor. It provides a thorough review of quality audit principles and standards.

Mizuno, Shigeru, ed. *Management for Quality Improvement: The 7 New QC Tools.* Cambridge, Mass.: Productivity Press, 1988.

This book explains seven new quality tools that promote a higher level of quality control activity, total coordination of the workplace, and creative planning.

Ozeki, Kazuo, and Tetavicki Asalea. *Handbook of Quality Tools: The Japanese Approach.* Norwalk, Conn.: Productivity Press, 1990.

Part I of this book offers a discussion of the management aspects of quality. Part II deals with the seven basic quality control tools and five new tools.

Perigord, Michel. *Achieving Total Quality Management: A Program for Action.* Norwalk, Conn.: Productivity Press, 1991.

Based on the author's experiences, the book presents a series of steps for achieving a successful quality program.

Rosander, A. C. *The Quest for Quality in Services.* Milwaukee: American Society for Quality Control, 1989.

This book tells how to plan and start a quality program in a service company. The author describes the work of five experts and their influence on services, the eight kinds of knowledge needed for improvement of quality, and how to conduct a continual customer opinion survey.

Rothery, Brian. *ISO 9000.* Brookfield, Vt.: Grower Publishing Co., 1991.

Provides a comprehensive guide for selecting an appropriate ISO Standard and preparing for registration. Discusses future directions, including a service version.

Walton, Mary. *Deming Management at Work.* New York: Putnam Publishing Group, 1990.

This book offers practical applications of the Deming management method. Six successful organizations are profiled in their use of the method.

Walton, Mary. *The Deming Management Method.* Cincinnati: Association for Quality and Participation, 1986.

Explains Deming's fourteen points and examines the results attained by some of the most innovative U.S. companies.

Zemke, Ron, and Dick Scaaf. *The Service Edge: 101 Companies That Profit from Customer Care.* New York: NAL Books, 1989.

This book profiles 101 companies that benefit from superior service and provides analysis of successful service policies and procedures.

Index